UP
IN YOUR
BUSINESS

THE ART OF PRODUCTIVITY

UP
IN YOUR
BUSINESS

THE ART OF PRODUCTIVITY

MARK JOHNSON

Up In Your Business, The Art Of Productivity
Mark D. Johnson

For information regarding permission to use content
contained in this book, speaking engagements, or bulk
purchases, contact: coach.mj@icloud.com

Up In Your Business, The Art Of Productivity is a
trademark of Mark D. Johnson

Manufactured & Printed in the United States of America.

ISBN- 978-1-63625-019-9

ENDORSEMENTS

"Mark - over the years - has produced a body of work for productivity and systems to drive business results. I know you will enjoy these short stories as much as I did."

Ben Hess, Co-Founder CoRecruit and Managing Partner of Thirdpool Recruiting Services.

"A strategic thinker and sharp business mind who has a knack for breaking the complex down to practical steps we can all apply. You'll benefit from the short stories outlined in this latest release from Mark."

Joseph Schottland, Innovatus Capital Partners

I enjoyed this quick read from Mark. As a strategic partner with KNOCK, Mark understands productivity and business systems. You will find practical advice to achieve any outcome in the pages that follow.

Sean Black, CEO Knock

Mark is known for his ability to break the complex down into related action steps; he not only inspires small business owners; he gives them practical steps to apply each day. I enjoyed these short stories and will be sharing the insights he has written on the following pages.

Jim Kelly, CEO Lone Wolf Technologies

Mark understands the difference between motion and action. They sound similar, yet they are different. I enjoy his work because it is thought-provoking, yet more than anything, it's ACTION-provoking.

Dr. Shane Creado, Author & board-certified
psychiatrist and sleep medicine physician

Mark and I share a similar philosophy...do the right thing for the person you are serving. Whether they are across the table or across the video call, do the right thing. And that's what you will get from this collection of action-packed short stories.

Steve Harney, Founder of Keeping Current Matters

Mark is a servant leader and one who pours into his agents. This collection of blogs has helped many achieve greater levels of production and satisfaction in their careers.

Steve Murray, President, and Founder of Real Trends

DEDICATION

Glory be to him whose power, working in us, can do infinitely more than we can ask or imagine.

~ Ephesians 3:20

This book is dedicated to the 2,400 sales professionals, 88 business partners, and 40 staff members that I so proudly serve. They take the risk, bear the challenges, and reap the rewards of their efforts daily. No business is easy and running a professional real estate practice is no exception. I am forever grateful for the gift of serving them.

Plus, a dedication to Charles Deming – the father of continuous improvement. This is a process I've learned to follow and has served me well, so thank you, Charles. And finally, to my good friend Neil Shusterman who motivated me to write my two books and in a late-night texting rally helped lead me to the name "Up In Your Business!"

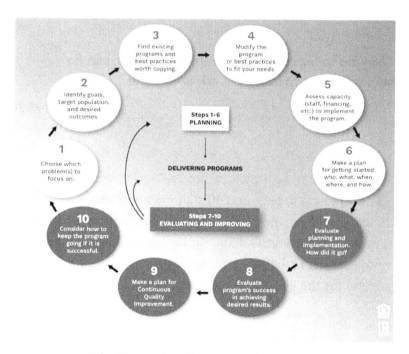

The Demming Process In My View

FORWARD

What if the common thinking about what makes us productive is all wrong? Hard work is undoubtedly important, yet science shows us peak performance is more than hard work; it's also the ideal combination of quality sleep, time off, consistent exercise, and proper nutrition.

#WinTheDay and #GSD (get stuff done) are hashtags I'm known for. You see, as a scientist, as a student of success, the most productive people I've studied focus on process goals.

Process goals are different than outcome or performance goals. Process goals are those activities consistently executed daily to create the best outcomes. Process goals are the milestones that you can completely control. A process goal is an outcome that is based on specific actions and tasks that you complete. Setting a process goal means you have to identify what you actually have to do to achieve a larger purpose.

Another common trait of highly productive people I've observed is action – they simply get stuff done. #GSD. Here is what I know **"the business world rewards action, not thought."** So, in this compilation of the blogs I've written over the past three years, you will see a strong bias towards taking action. There are even three actions to take when you don't know what to do!

And finally, what you will find in the pages that follow are the four things I've found that is needed to produce any outcome:

- Growth Mindset at the base
- A game plan comes next
- Followed by skills
- And topped off by the right tools

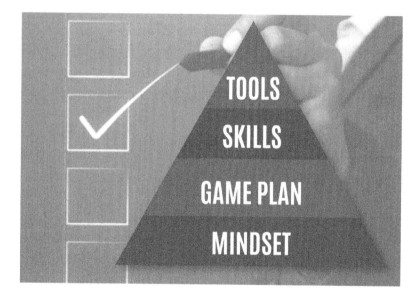

Let's get after it, and I trust you will find value in the pages that follow. Let me know if something you read here resonates with you and activates you into getting into a positive momentum.

TABLE OF CONTENTS

WHAT IS YOUR PROMISE?

"I don't trust words, I trust actions."

~ Mark Johnson

Consumers will be loyal to brands that deliver what they need – dependability, service, exceptional service, or extraordinary value.

When a brand consistently meets a need, it becomes a brand promise and becomes its identity. FedEx, for example, the brand promise is **"when it absolutely positively has to be there overnight."** FedEx consistently delivers on its promise, which creates an influential association, bond of trust, and loyalty with consumers. As the CEO of your real estate practice, YOU are and critical extension of the JPAR brand.

The financial stakes of a transaction have a proportional effect on brand loyalty. Consumers have far less to lose by trying another brand of candy than they do another brand of a real estate agent or lender. As a service professional, you are the brand, which you enhance and solidify each time you meet and exceed your clients' expectations.

If you have locked in your clients' trust (and their willingness to refer you) through brand loyalty, you have a massive advantage over your competition.

How do you achieve brand loyalty? Consistently deliver your brand promise, and do it better than your competitors. Sporadic high performance will not cut it — EVERY customer must have the same great experience. Instead of chasing the next technology tool or widget, think about your service delivery.

Rate your service delivery on a scale of 1 (low) to 10 (high). What will it take to be a 10?

Knowing your customers' anxiety points is critical to achieving a strong brand promise. After all, consumers want brands that meet their needs, but not if the experience is painful.

Action – what action can you take?

Ask your customers this week what worries them most about the transaction. Then let them know what you will do to address their concerns.

That's one solid way to build brand trust and loyalty.

Our Promise – at JPAR is to – exceed expectations. Personal Representation, Powerful Resources, Proven Results. Delivering on that promise will serve you well.

#WinTheDay

THE QUANTUM LEAP STRATEGY

Imagination is the most potent force in the universe.

~ Albert Einstein

Consider this:
- Today's smartphone has the same computing power as the whole US government in 1983
- 3D printing is the only technology where a more complex object doesn't cost more to make
- The average lifespan of an S&P 500 company has gone from 67 years to 12 years today
- Autonomous driving cars will prevent 30,000 road deaths in the US alone

Exponential Growth

Exponential growth does not just apply to technology, large or small firms. Exponential growth applies to you and me.

One of the most influential books I've read. The book is just 36 pages long yet is packed with practical insight and action creating motivation. It's called _You Squared by Price Pritchett_. It is an instruction manual for taking a quantum leap in your business and life.

Pritchett states, "we don't have to be content with incremental, gradual change through the application of hard work. Rather, we are capable of an explosive jump in performance at an accelerated rate, and it requires less effort." How?

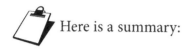 Here is a summary:

Quit Trying Harder – Trying harder only produces incremental gains. A quantum shift is an elegant solution requiring less effort.

Ignore Conventional Approaches – A quantum leap requires an abrupt change in behavior. It requires finesse over effort, simplicity over complexity, a new paradigm, and a fresh perspective.

Think Beyond What Common Sense Would Allow – Quantum leaps require "uncommon sense." Rethink your thinking. Violate the boundaries of the probable.

Suspend Disbelief – Act as if your success is for certain and proceed boldly.

Focus On Ends Rather Than Means – It is crucial to have a clear picture of what you want to accomplish. Solutions will appear. Draw the map as you go.

Rely On Unseen Forces – When you focus on the clear picture of what you want to accomplish and move confidently toward it, unexpected and unknown resources materialize.

Choose A Different Set Of Rules – You can never avoid risk; you can only choose which risks you will take. Risk believing in yourself.

Trust In The Power Of The Pursuit – Dreams begin to crystallize into reality when pursued because the world behaves differently when you go after what you want.

Seek Failure – Unless you are willing to fail, you will never have the opportunity to test the limits of what you are capable of accomplishing.

Get Uncomfortable – Quantum leaps jerk you out of your comfort zone. If you aren't experiencing discomfort, the risk you are taking probably isn't worthy of you.

Open Your Gifts – Unused gifts are waiting to play a role in your quantum leap; open them.

Fall In Love – Create a dramatic dream that goes beyond the 'reasonable,' and then allow it to become your "magnificent obsession."

Make Your Move Before You Are Ready – You don't prepare for a quantum leap; you make it… and then you fine-tune as you go.

Look Inside For The Opportunity – Everything else that's needed comes from *inside* you, not from anything outside you.

If you choose to take the leap, I invite you to consider what business area is holding you back?

Maybe it's hiring an assistant; perhaps it's outsourcing that new digital ad campaign you desire but don't have the skills or time to pursue; perhaps it's delegating your files to a transaction coordinator? Whatever it is, one or more of the principles Pritchett presents, I suspect, resonates with you, so… just do it!

Take the leap and see you and your business take a quantum leap.

#WinTheDay

ASK A BETTER QUESTION

The power of questions is the basis of all human progress.

~ Indira Gandhi

As you read this, how many days remain in the year? Maximizing the time you have remaining starts with 5 quality questions.

Five Quality Questions:
1. What are the most important lessons you learned about yourself and your business this year?
2. As a result of question #1, what is your plan to course correct and close stronger than you started?
3. What new disciplines do you need to start NOW and master to create the most successful close to the year? Who will hold you accountable?
4. What new skills will you need to master to compete in the next 90 days?
   - Marketing to create more appointments.
   - Upgrade your listing presentation to WIN every listing.
   - Start a killer buyer capabilities presentation to WIN every buyer.
   - Handling objections.

5. What new technology or lead generation tools will you master to bring your business to a new level?

There you have it, 5 quality questions that will lead you to a stronger close to this year or any year.

What's your answer?
What's your next step?

#WinTheDay

SUCCESS IN REAL ESTATE SALES

"Opportunities don't happen. You create them."

~ Chris Grosser

The most expensive piece of real estate is the six inches between your right and left ear. It's what you create in this space that determines your success. A growth mindset is listed as #1 on my list of things needed to drive your success. The four things required, in order of importance to create any outcome are:

#1 – A growth mindset
#2 – A solid game plan
#3 – Skills – selling & marketing skills
#4 – Enabling tools and resources

A growth mindset
Our mindsets exist on a continuum from fixed to growth, and although we'd like always to have a growth mindset, the reality is that we can pivot back and forth. The goal is to recognize fixed mindset elements in ourselves and then adjust along the way. Progress not perfection or said another way continuous improvement.

You can have the best game plan and strategy, yet if you aren't in a peak performance mindset, the obstacles will be harder to overcome.

"You only have control over three things in your life — the thoughts you think, the images you visualize, and the actions you take. How you use these three things determines everything you experience."

~ Jack Canfield

A solid game plan
A game plan tells you the what, the how, the when, and the why of achieving a stated goal. A game plan is all about taking control of – designing, not reacting – to the business.

I use the business mastery module of the real estate playbook that start with:

- How many consumers do you want to serve?
- How many conversations do you need to create one appointment, and how many appointments are required to create one Sale?

First, I challenge our associates to stop and think; second, write it down; and third, to be logical. Business is just math; for example: how many conversations are needed to create one new appointment? WHO do I need to be to create those appointments?

Selling and business operations skills
You will need the skills to execute your game plan. One of those skills is effectively automating, delegating, or eliminating parts of the business that aren't in your zone of genius. Like the 15

hours of paperwork required in the average transaction, we find it best to delegate that to a coordinator like www.jpartc.com so you can work on prospecting, appointments, and negotiations.

Inc. published a study of the five critical skills needed for business success:

#1 Selling and marketing skills
#2 Planning and lead generation skills
#3 Customer service skills
#4 Communication skills (www.jparcode.com)
#5 Curiosity

When the only limit you have in your skills is what you can imagine and apply, just about anything is possible.

So many of us are trained to think hard work is all that is required. Hard work is essential, yet without adequate sleep, a good diet, exercise, and time away, our productivity is not optimized.

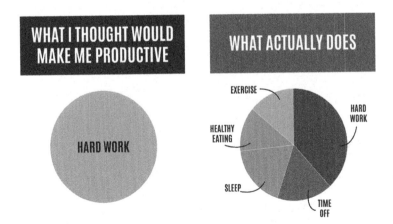

Enabling tools and resources
I could give you a Ferrari, yet if you did not have the skills to compete in the race, you'd lose or, worse yet, crash!

I've seen the Sure Sale Program offered at JPAR out of Texas; it's an innovative approach that allows the consumer to choose traditional selling, trading the home (swapping) or a direct buyout. Consider this:

- A carpenter's skills don't change when he switches from a hammer to a pneumatic nailer. You hire him for his building skills, not the number of hours he's spent swinging a hammer.
- A writer doesn't forget everything she knows just because she switches from a typewriter to a computer, changes from a yellow legal pad to a Moleskine notebook, or even switches favorite brands of pen. You read her books because she knows how to tell a good story.
- Computer programmers don't lose their skills and experience just because they got a new computer.

That's why our all great approaches to training reinforce these five factors in order of importance:

#1 – A growth mindset
#2 – A solid game plan
#3 – Skills – selling & marketing skills
#4 – Enabling tools and resources

It's great to have aspirations, yet it's crucial to take significant actions. If you want to have a better outcome, guess what?

You will have to hold yourself accountable to take the steps that move the needle.

The five steps outlined here will ensure you achieve any outcome you desire.

What actions are you committed to taking?

#WinTheDay

BACK TO BASICS

In times of life crisis, whether wildfires or smoldering stress, the first thing I do is go back to basics... am I eating right, am I getting enough sleep, am I getting some physical and mental exercise every day.

~ Edward Albert

Fundamentals matter… let me share a story.

It was July of 1961, and the 38 members of the Green Bay Packers football team were gathered together for the first day of training camp. The previous season had ended with a heartbreaking defeat when the Packers squandered a lead late in the 4th quarter and lost the NFL Championship to the Philadelphia Eagles.

The Green Bay players had been thinking about this brutal loss for the entire off-season, and now, finally, training camp had arrived, and it was time to get to work. The players were eager to advance their game to the next level and start working on the details to win a championship.

Their coach, Vince Lombardi, had a different idea.

Lombardi took nothing for granted. He began a tradition of starting from scratch, assuming that the players were blank

slates who carried over no knowledge from the year before...
He began with the most introductory statement of all:

Gentlemen, this is a football!

Lombardi was coaching a group of three dozen professional athletes who, just months prior, had come within minutes of winning the biggest prize their sport could offer. And yet, he started from the very beginning.

Lombardi's systematic coverage of the fundamentals continued throughout the training camp. Each player reviewed how to block and tackle. They opened up the playbook and started on page one. His team would become the best in the league at the tasks everyone else took for granted.

Six months later, the Green Bay Packers beat the New York Giants 37-0 to win the NFL Championship.

Is this your season to get back to basics?

FUNDAMENTAL ONE: PICK UP YOUR PHONE
Schedule time this month to contact your database and check-in. Find out what's new and remind them that you are never too busy for them. Be ready to with some current market facts, how things are going in your area, any new community events or initiatives. A great source of content is available from my good friends at Keeping Current Matters.

FUNDAMENTAL TWO: THROW A PARTY
The post-holiday party let down is real! There's always a reason to get your past clients, prospects, and friends together to show

them appreciation. You could host a charity event, valentine's day event, or even a March madness party. It does not need to be complicated, just fun.

FUNDAMENTAL THREE: WRITE A NOTE

A lost art is writing a personal note! Writing a note establishes a more personal level of connection. Even if you just write something as easy as "Happy February!" A handwritten note will go a long way in keeping you top of mind.

FUNDAMENTAL FOUR: STOP BY WITH A GIFT

Face-to-face is powerful with clients at any time of the year. I once worked with an agent that always had boy and girl gift baskets in the car that he dropped off anywhere he saw the "stork!" Get creative and stop by with anything of value, and you will not only build a relationship yet also stay top of mind.

A hope and a wish are NOT sales strategies… consistency is. Are you leaving too much to chance or getting consistent on the fundamentals?

The football season may be over, yet that does not mean you can't have a winning season by focusing on the fundamentals.

#WinTheDay

5 LESSONS FROM THE DEATH CRAWL SCENE IN "FACING THE GIANTS

"Brock, I need you. God's gifted you with the ability of leadership. Don't waste it."

~ Grant Taylor

How are you facing YOUR giant?

Consider this: Facing your giant is about the continuum of moving your mindset from fixed to growth mode.

I'm reminded that our perception, surroundings, and beliefs get in the way of victory and success too often. Or, stated another way, the meaning we assign to things becomes the lens through which we see the world.

Lesson 1 – *Don't Write A Bad Month Off As A Loss Before It's Over*
You never know how that next sales call, the next text interaction, the next phone conversation, or the upcoming coffee meeting will turn out until it's over.

It's so easy to get discouraged when you are having a bad day or a bad month. Sales are off, morale is low, and you feel like crawling under a rock. It's so easy to set yourself on "cruise control" for the remainder of the month and just focus on next month. While this can be a good thing to improve your performance for next month, writing off this month as a loss before it's even over is the worst thing you can do.

If you have not seen the movie, the team ends up having a pretty successful season. It was not astounding, but if they had just given up halfway through, they would not have seen the level of success they achieved that season. The same can be said about your sales performance too. It's not over until it's over.

Staying in inspired action despite the circumstances surrounding you is the definition of mental toughness. Mental toughness is developed with exercise, just like a muscle.

Lesson 2 – *Once You Hit A Goal, Don't Give Up*
In the scene, Coach Grant blindfolded Brock. After all, he didn't want him to give up once he hit the 50-yard line because he knew that he could exceed that goal. On the other hand, Brock didn't even believe that he could get to the 50-yard line in the first place.

Often, we see a sales quota or a bonus level and decide that it is our goal, and once we hit that goal, we can just give up and focus on the next month. This scene shatters that belief. If Brock had just given up at the 50, he never would have believed that he could make it the entire field. Much like in sales, if you stop at $10k in sales because that's the goal in your head, you could be missing out on $20k month or better.

In a separate post, I've written about PROCESS goals, PERFORMANCE goals, and OUTCOME goals. Research shows those that focus on PROCESS goals achieve the OUTCOME more frequently than those that focus on outcome goals.

Lesson 3 – *Give Your VERY Best*

We all go on listing appointments, buyer presentations, call, text, or message prospects and go through a script. We handle the objections and do everything like we were taught. Yet, if you just do that, you might be a successful salesperson and might have a good month. What separates the good from the great are the salespeople who look at themselves after a call – whether a sale is made or not – and can say, *"that was not my absolute very best, I can do better."*

Those who learn how to give their absolute very best are the ones who are always at the top of the performance charts. I call it good, better, best. What was good; what could be better; what was the best? An excellent exercise for continuous improvement.

You see, there is a difference between giving something your best and giving something your *very* best. If Brock just gave it his best, he might have made it to the 75-yard line. Towards the end, when he was in extreme pain and was hurting, the coach Grant was screaming in his face for him to fight on and keep going. It didn't matter how much Brock was hurting or how tired he was. Much to Brock's amazement – and his teammates – he was able to do the entire field, but only by giving it his absolute very best.

Lesson 4 – *You Inspire Others When You Perform At Your Best*

At the beginning of this scene, Brock's teammates laughed at him as he attempted to make it to the 50-yard line with Jeremy on his back. In the end, they were speechless, and they stood up in respect. If, as a top performer, you are exceeding your goals and are showing others that it *can* be done, people will follow suit and will start to believe that they can do it too. It will garner respect and will turn a joke and defeated environment into a serious and inspired one.

You can be an inspiration and an unstoppable force for good for others in your community.

Lesson 5 – *No Matter What, Refuse To Walk Around Defeated*
When top performers walk around with grim faces and an obvious feeling of defeat, it will permeate throughout the office, and everyone will start to believe that they, too, are losers who can't win. At the beginning of the clip, Brock openly said that he didn't think that they could win. You can see that his teammates believed it. After the death crawl, it was an entirely different environment.

As a top performer, are you a negative Nelly, or are you rallying the others around you? Walking around defeated before it's even over only guarantees that you will lose. In the movie, even though they lost their best performer and had six straight years of losing, they could have a successful season.

HOW ARE YOU FACING YOUR GIANT?
We recently turned our training and technology offerings on its head. You can attack projects with vigor or crawl under a rock. You can be overwhelmed or step back and set a plan; you can do nothing or break it down into small parts and plan to win.

For the rest of this year, will you give your VERY best?
In the end, we all know the CHOICE is yours.
You and I have too much to offer to play small.

Who is in? Let's go!

#WinTheDay

RESOLUTIONS SUCK!

Always bear in mind that your resolution to succeed is more important than any one thing.

~ Abraham Lincoln

At the start of each year, we make a resolution; it's tradition. Yet come March, are you ever asked, "So, how are those New Year's resolutions working out for you? What if you set a monthly reminder?

The dream is that our goals and resolutions lead us to new horizons and higher ground. They can give our eyes a focus, our mind an aim, and our strength a purpose. Without the positive pull forward of a goal, we risk remaining forever stagnant, or even worse, sucked into a backward spiral.

So why is it so hard to keep and reach some resolutions, some goals?

We have all felt the excitement that comes with setting a new goal, but then, as time progresses, excitement can morph into anxiety. This is because we face the reality that we are so far from our goal and have no framework or strategy to get there.

So how do you overcome life's hurdles and personal mental roadblocks to reach your BIG goals?

Well, first, a blinding flash of the obvious: When you set goals for yourself, it is essential that they motivate you: this means making sure that they are necessary to you and that there is value in achieving them.

Motivation is the key to achieving goals. Set goals that relate to the high priorities in your life. If the goal is truly not important to you, and you can't tie it back to why it's meaningful, your chances of success diminish. Yet wait, there's more:

THE REALITY IS, THERE'S A SCIENCE TO GOAL SETTING

In over 650 studies completed with over 50,000 participants, scientists analyzed what worked best when goal setting. Overall, individuals who focused on *Process Goals* had more success in reaching their goals than those who simply set Performance or Outcome Goals.

What is the difference between an outcome goal, a performance goal, and a process goal?

An outcome goal is one that isn't really under your control. Instead, it's based on outside circumstances. For example, if your goal is to the #1 selling agent in your market, that's a goal that is found not only on your numbers but also on the numbers from other agents in your market.

Performance goals are personal achievement goals. They are the building blocks that help you reach your outcome goal. A good performance goal example is to "beat my record of 21 homes sold in a year.

Process goals are entirely under your control and are composed of the things you do daily, like habits and routines. Think of these as the small steps you take to get to your performance and outcome goals every day. An example of a process goal would be to "spend 60 minutes prospecting daily" or "40 minutes of cardio work."

So, there you have it, the science behind more effective goal setting. Create a goal that is important to you, and one you can be reminded frequently as to why you are pursuing it. Then, break those outcome goals down to the daily activities, the daily processes.

Now your likelihood of achievement is dramatically improved.

#WinTheDay

THE PAIN OF REGRET
OR THE PAIN OF DISCIPLINE

"Of all the words of mice and men, the saddest are, "It might have been."

~ Kurt Vonnegut

As many of us are working on those New Year resolutions and what's possible. Here's a quick question for you to consider:

"Do you prefer the pain of discipline OR the pain of regret?"

Research shows that we regret those things we have not done MORE than we do the things we have done. Can you relate?

I've experienced personally and observed in others that procrastination blocks us from creating the business and life we want. You already know, the main reason we procrastinate is that taking action can cause us a certain amount of "pain, a certain amount of discomfort."

Coaching clients have shared with me, "I'm avoiding undertaking certain tasks because of the risk of shame, vulnerability, or failure. Taking action means we might be making a mistake, or we might fail. Let's face it; it's easier not to take action and avoid the pain of looking less than perfect. Thus, many of us instinctively retreat to our comfort zone and miss creating our ideal business. Basically, in trying to protect ourselves from failure, it's easier to erect our barriers to success. Can you relate? If you've ever been in this place – as I have – how do you get out?

Psychologists call this a strategy of self-sabotaging. Research shows by creating impediments that make success less likely, we protect our sense of self-competence. And believe it or not, we as humans **tend to do this more when the stakes are the highest.**

So how do we procrastinate less and take action more? Practice. Practice taking action faster and more often. Get an accountability partner and join a mastermind group. By taking more small steps that lead to bigger steps, you'll build the "take action muscle." By creating an accountability partner and mastermind group, you'll have others who can help you discern what is an excuse and what's not.

CONSIDER THESE 5 ACTION STEPS:

1. **Remember, a goal is NOT a system.** A system will produce what a system will produce nothing less, nothing more. For example, losing 10 pounds by September 1st is a GOAL. Learning how to change your eating habits is a SYSTEM. See the difference?

2. **Make your goal tangible and specific.** "Grow my business" sounds great but is also meaningless. "Land five new clients a month" allows you to determine exactly what you need to

do to land those clients. Always set a goal that helps you to work backward and create a process designed to achieve it. It's impossible to know exactly what to do every day when you don't know precisely what you want to achieve.

3. **Make it matter to you!** If you want to get in better shape, so other people will think you look better at the pool this summer, you're unlikely to follow through. Ultimately, who cares what other people think?

Yet, if you want to get in better shape because you want to feel better, feel better about yourself, set an example for your kids, or prove something to yourself...then, you're much more likely to stick with it. Now your goal has meaning–not to your doctor, not to strangers at the pool, but to you.

4. **Make it positive.** "Stop criticizing other people in meetings" is a great goal, but it's an opposing goal. It's a lot harder to give up or stop doing something than embrace a new and positive challenge. For example, setting a goal like "stop eating sweets" means you constantly have to choose to avoid temptation, and since willpower is often a finite resource, why put yourself in a position of constantly needing to choose?

When you pick positive goals, you'll be working to become something new rather than avoid being something you no longer wish to be.

5. **Focus on the process, the DAILY process.** All incredibly successful people I've worked with have one thing in common... they set a goal and then focus all their attention

on the process necessary to achieve that goal. Sure, the goal is still out there. But what they care about most is what they need to do today–and when they accomplish that, they feel happy about today.

So, I'll ask again, do you prefer the pain of discipline OR the pain of regret? The choice is yours.

#WinTheDay

TIRED OF NOT GETTING WHAT YOU WANT?

Growth is painful. Change is painful. Yet nothing is as painful as staying stuck where you don't belong.

~ Mandy Hale

Ever wonder why so many of us have to hit rock bottom before we find a breakthrough? Let me explain; from working with others, I've discovered a pattern. Typically after a huge disappointment, fear of failure disappears. When the fear of failure disappears, taking a positive action becomes easier.

Once a major low is hit, the realization that any action taken must lead to something better. Think about that for a moment, "any positive action taken leads to something better!" Make sense?

THE PROBLEM.
Waiting for a major breakdown to get to a breakthrough.

- *Maybe you're satisfied with mediocrity?*
- *Maybe you believe you will fail*
- *Maybe you care a little too much about the opinion of others?*
- *Maybe you are addicted to worry, the past, or to drama?*

- *Maybe you let overwhelm, and distractions get in the way*
- *Maybe you succumb to those five words that kill more dreams: "I don't feel like it!"*

For the vast majority of folks I've worked with, the answer to the question, "why don't you do what you have to do to get what you want?" Can be summarized in 5 dream killing words:

I don't feel like it!

And that feeling stops you from taking positive action, keeps you from being consistent. It's the one reason you're not getting what you want. Your feelings overpower your commitment. Your feelings overpower your ability to take positive action.

The Solution.

Act opposite your feelings.

The story of Mario Lemieux:

Many athletes have played through or returned from life-threatening illnesses. Others have come back from debilitating injuries that would have forced mere mortals to give the game up. And then there is Mario Lemieux, 17 National Hockey League seasons with the Pittsburgh Penguins from 1984 to 2006, and the assuming ownership in 1999.

He is the only man to have his name on the Stanly Cup as both a player and an owner.

Yet he not only suffered from Hodgkin's lymphoma he also endured chronic back pain, spinal disc herniation, chronic tendinitis of the hip flexor muscle. His pain at times was so severe that other people had to tie his skates for him.

Lemieux won three Most Valuable Player awards in the NHL and six times was its leading scorer with his puck-handling dexterity, long reach, and accurate shot.

Lemieux is the only player to average more than two points a game (2.01). His goal-scoring percentage of .823 (613 goals in 745 games) is the best for players with 150 games.

I know there were many times Mario "didn't feel like it," yet his commitment was greater than his feelings.

When your commitments overpower your feelings, that's when breakthroughs begin.

When you take action despite your feelings, that's when breakthroughs begin.

So, who's in charge: **YOU** or your feelings?

#WinTheDay

WHY DO MOST EFFORTS
TO CHANGE FAIL?

"Everyone thinks of changing the world, but no one thinks of changing himself."

~ Leo Tolstoy

According to Harvard professor Dr. John Paul Kotter – and confirmed by my coaching experience – efforts to change fail due to a lack of a STRONG sense of URGENCY. In his book, "*A Sense Of Urgency*," Kotter states:

Change efforts most often fail when those desiring to change do not create a high enough sense of urgency for making a challenging leap in a new direction. Urgency, urgency is key. Urgency is the state of mind that creates IMMEDIATE action in your new direction.

Once you have determined your desire, take action. Any action. A small step, a medium step, or a massive step. Taking action and taking more action is the ONE THING we must all learn to cultivate to achieve higher levels of success.

If you believe what you have in mind will make a difference, I just have two questions.

- What are you waiting for?
- What's holding you back?

Whatever it is, push through it today and TAKE ACTION.

Share with someone right now the action step you are committed to taking… and ask them to help hold you accountable.

#WinTheDay

WHAT TO DO WHEN YOU DON'T KNOW WHAT TO DO

"The secret of getting ahead is getting started. The secret to getting started is breaking your overwhelming tasks into small manageable tasks and then starting on the first one."

~Mark Twain

Because of work pressure and the need to produce results, it's easy to get overwhelmed. That feeling can quickly produce uncertainty. You become afraid to act, and instead, it's easy to worry and spend an excessive amount of time thinking through worst-case scenarios, something I am pretty good at.

If you are in a situation where you feel overwhelmed and don't know what course to take, *"just do the next right thing."*

Michael Hyatt shared three steps to consider in doing the "next right thing."

1. **Forget about the ultimate outcome.** The truth is you have less control over the outcome than you think. You can undoubtedly influence it, but you can't control it. Besides, before you ever get to the final destination, many of the variables will change. Projects and deals have a way of

unfolding over time. There will be problems—and resources—you can't see now.

2. **Instead, focus on the next right action.** Since worrying about the outcome is unproductive, try to think about the next actions to move you forward. This is far more accessible than something in the distant future. For example, as a writer, I can worry about whether or not my book will become a bestseller, or I can make sure that I am fully prepped for the interview I have scheduled today.

3. **And do something now!** This is key. Something is better than nothing. Too often, we think that we have to have clarity about how it will all turn out. In my experience, I rarely have this. But, as I move toward the destination, making course corrections as necessary, I experience clarity. Therefore, it is important to get off the sidelines and into the game.

I don't know about you, but I tend to become paralyzed in these situations. But, not anymore.

#WinTheDay

SO HOW CONSISTENT ARE YOU RIGHT NOW?

"It's not what we do once in a while that shapes our lives. It's what we do consistently."

~ Tony Robbins

When you are inconsistent, nothing works. Here's what I know: sales professionals who are consistently setting and going on new appointments are producing more results, period. These professionals are consistent and disciplined in their daily routine of prospecting and marketing.

Consistency. Social media does not work if you are not consistent; geographic farming does not work if you are not consistent; repeat and referral systems do not work if you are not consistent; open houses do not work if you are inconsistent; online leads do not work if you are not consistent.

Show me something in your life or business that works when you are inconsistent. Anything you are going to do, the more consistent you are with your mindset, your attitude, your approach, your expectation, your strategy, and your tactics, the more predictable the result.

> Bottom line: when you are consistent, everything works when you are inconsistent, nothing works.

So my question is, what have you been inconsistent with? What has that inconsistency cost you financially, cost you emotionally, cost you physically?

I'd submit the action that we can all be more consistent in setting and going on more appointments.

- We **CANNOT** control the market.
- We **CAN** control ourselves, our thoughts, and our actions.

Next Steps:
1. Make an appointment setting goal for the next two weeks and share it with an accountability partner.
2. Gather your past client list, all of your past leads, open house registers, and people you know and start making appointments today.
3. Be CONSISTENT. List the 1, 2, or 3 things that you must do consistently that will propel your business forward.

#WinTheDay

7 STEPS TO AN APPOINTMENT SETTING BREAKTHROUGH

"In the end, someone or something always gives up. It is either you give up and quit, or the obstacle or failure gives up and makes way for your success to come through."

~ Idowu Koyenikan

Stop and reflect for a moment. How would your business be impacted if you went on at least one or more appointments each workday?

Here's what I know: sales professionals who are setting and going on new APPOINTMENTS are PRODUCING, period. Those that are consistent and disciplined in their daily routines win the day.

Consider this:

- We CANNOT control the market.
- We CANNOT control what others think.
- We CAN control our business process.
- We CAN control our thoughts, behaviors, and routines.

So, why is it that some sales professionals are succeeding wildly today while other agents are getting out of the business?

What separates those who are still making sales from those who are not?

What is the key to succeeding in this market or any market for that matter?

This posting intends to give you specific ideas and techniques that will lead to a breakthrough in the number of appointments you set. Let's begin by defining what an appointment is, and then we will look at seven ways to set an appointment a day.

WHAT IS AN APPOINTMENT?

APPOINTMENTS are any meetings that will positively impact your business. Specifically:

- Sitting face-to-face with a motivated seller (listing presentation)
- Working with a buyer who wants to buy
- Previewing a motivated For Sale By Owner property
- A face-to-face meeting with a Past Client, a Center of Influence, or anyone who can refer you to business
- Meeting with potential investor clients or directors of HR involved in executive moves

Again, I'll ask how would your business be impacted if you went on at least one appointment each workday? How would that feel?

Check out these 7 steps that can inspire you to create an appointment setting breakthrough:

1. Focus Daily on Setting Appointments

Some agents focus on the amount of time they engage in some form of lead generation each day. Some focus on the number of people they contact each day, and some focus on the number of leads they generate.

Top producers focus on:
- Setting great appointments
- Getting contracts signed

2. Create A Definition of an Appointment that Serves You

If your definition of an appointment is something like, "I only meet with sellers who will list with me today at 2:00 P.M. for 25% under fair market value and 9% commission," you will likely find yourself with an empty appointment book!

If you want a full appointment book, refer to the definition outlined above and start setting more appointments today.

3. Affirm That You Set Appointments Daily

Affirm that you will set an appointment each day. Say this simple affirmation constantly throughout the day:

"I set two or more appointments each day!!"

Consider this easy exercise and watch how it can positively affect your mindset and results.

4. Carry Your Best leads with You At All Times

One way to do this is to put your best leads on 3×5 index cards and carry them with you all day long. Or enter them into your Smart Phones note or reminder app. Or use a CRM with mobile capability. Have a system as we know a system will produce what a system will produce, nothing less, nothing more. What does your current system produce?

The key is to call your leads constantly throughout the day. Consider **calling your leads three separate times each day** to increase the probability of reaching them and setting an appointment. Call them first thing in the morning, try it again around lunchtime do your last attempt at the end of the day. You cannot overcall your leads. Even better, consider using a tool like REAL CONTACT to streamline your process.

5. Know Your Automatic Shot
Your "automatic shot" is the source of business you know you can count on if you really needed a deal. We all have areas in which we excel over others, and we all have sources that are particularly favorable for us. You must know what it is for you.

Ask yourself this question: *"If you absolutely had to set an appointment today, who would you call?"* The answer to this question will define who or what your automatic shot is. Make sure to take your automatic shot every day!

6. Learn 5-7 Basic Closes to Improve Confidence
Skills and confidence are critical in this market. JPAR is now more than ever focused on assisting our agents and teams in improving their skills. We are surrounded by like-minded professionals that invest the time in learning the scripts and objection handlers necessary to confidently set appointments with ease. Let's work to enhance your closing and objection handling skills so you can add one.

7. Be Unattached to How and Where Your Next Appointment Comes From

The key here is to remain focused on the fact that you intend to set at least one appointment each day. Once your intention is set, simply go about your business go follow your schedule… go out and do your lead generation and conversion.

> *"If I Am Always Shaking The Tree,*
> *An Apple Will Fall Somewhere!"*

So, there you have seven ways to set at least one appointment a day. I want to encourage you to shift your focus and energy now.

Focus on:

1 – Finding your next appointment,

2 – Going to another appointment and

3 – Servicing your existing clients at the highest level.

Your ACTION STEPS:

- Make an appointment goal for the next two weeks and share it with an accountability partner.
- Gather all your past leads, open house registers, and people you know and start making appointments to meet – ask for tips on people they may know who needs to buy or sell. Use tools like – VERSE.IO – to streamline the follow up nurturing process.
- Consider creating a small appointment setting mastermind group that meets in your office weekly. Roleplay objections, practice your listing presentation, and critique each other, practice answering a buyer who asks: *"why should I use you?"*
- Once you have the appointment, consider what I learned from Jeff Bezos, CEO and founder of Amazon:

> *"We don't make money when we make a sale; we make money when we help someone make a purchase decision."*

My previous article topic may come in handy in planning your appointments. If you haven't seen my previous post on how to delegate, automate or eliminate, then check it out.

#WinTheDay

DELEGATE, AUTOMATE
OR ELIMINATE

"If you want to do a few small things right, do them yourself. If you want to do great things and make a big impact, learn to delegate."

~John C. Maxwell

Today's post is short and sweet. Sometimes those are the best.

You see, I've seen too many entrepreneurs follow this idea like it's some kind of commandment:

> **"If you want something done right, you have to do it yourself."**

Can you relate?

Imagine if you could delegate, automate or eliminate many of the tasks you're not good at, or dislike like booking appointments, marketing yourself, or running errands.

The result?

Creating more time to do what you are best at, love, and find important.

The key in the delegation is understanding and accepting that others simply won't do it like you. So, get over it! Have standards yet allow your team to run with it. When you do, what is possible in your personal productivity and life satisfaction? For real estate professionals, consider this as your JOB description:

- Planning
- Lead follow up
- Appointment setting
- Negotiations

Everything else delegate, automate, or eliminate!

Consider letting go of some of the things so you can spend more time in your genius zone. CrisMarie Campbell and Susan Clarke, Business Consultants and Authors of *The Beauty of Conflict*, recommend taking an honest look at how you are spending your time through a four-zone model.

What Is Your Zone?
- *Zone Of Incompetence* – you don't do these things well. Better to eliminate, automate, or delegate.
- *Zone of Competence* – you can do these things but don't like them much. Better to eliminate, automate, or delegate.
- *Zone of Excellence* – you are very good at these things. They bring you success, but they don't make your heart sing.
- *Zone of Genius* – you absolutely love doing these things, you do them well, and they give you the highest ratio of abundance and satisfaction to the amount of time invested.

For automation, consider "If This Then That." IFTTT is the freeway to get all your apps and devices talking to each other. Not everything on the internet plays nice, so IFTTT is on a mission to build a more connected world.

What type of work places you in your genius zone?

Do more of that.

Then consider what is left that you can delegate, automate, or eliminate this week.

This week is YOURS, **own it!**

#WinTheDay

WHAT MAKES YOU PRODUCTIVE?

"It's not always that we need to do more, but rather that we need to focus on less."

~ Nathan W. Morris

This just in: tough choices, making decisions tires your brain! We all make 100's of decisions a day, is that taxing?

Studies show your brain is just like a muscle. When your brain gets depleted, it's less effective. The compound effect of simple choices - like what groceries to buy this week - might lead us to procrastinate on that critical work project. A "tired" mind finds a path of least resistance in distracting leisure activities.

The solution? Set shifting, delegation, automation, or elimination, plus breaks and rest.

One culprit? Multitasking! If you think you're efficient when you perform three tasks at once, think again. It's very taxing on your brain.

Solution? "Set Shifting." This means wholly and consciously shifting your attention from one task to the next and focusing on the task at hand.

It sounds like an interview I need to set up with some experts – like Dr. Shane Creado. As of this writing, this is the #1 most viewed episode of Success Superstars. Episode #124 on YouTube.com/SuccessSuperStars

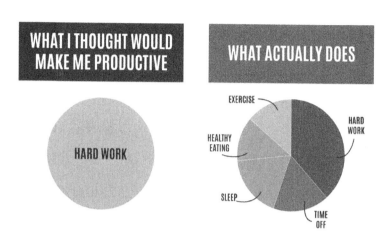

#WinTheDay

THE SILENT DREAM KILLER

"You see things; and you say, 'Why?' But I dream things that never were; and I say, 'Why not?'"

~ George Bernard Shaw

The five words that kill more dreams, more potential, and more happiness than any other five words spoken:

"I don't feel like it."

I'm not sure of your dream, yet I suspect for many of you it's more financial freedom, better health, stronger relationships, and more connectedness with your community. Yet let's face it, so many times when you are about to start something toward those dreams, the onslaught of excuses flood your mind like water gushing out of a broken pipe. The theme of these excuses always traces back to the same root: *"I don't feel like it."*

How many times have you said, "I don't feel like it?" How many times have you listened to that thought, allowing it to alter the course of your actions?

What if you could make a different choice?

Here is what I know, "I don't feel like it" is the universal human condition that silently kills dreams. Yet you and I don't have to accept this dream killer. We can all overcome the feeling and move powerfully towards our goals and dreams. It starts with intention: the intention to live on your terms, not the terms of your moods and feelings.

Next time you say to yourself, "I don't feel like it," consider this 4-step guide to snap out of that feeling and make a choice for different action.

 Step 1: Put Your Body In Motion

Emotion is created by motion. In other words, emotions are linked to movement in our bodies. Think about it: observe your posture when you are slouching or happy instead of when you are sad. Or what you look like when you are angry versus when you are elated. Our mothers were correct; proper posture means more than just looking good.

Try this little experiment, right now: stand up, smile and raise your hands above your head and say, "yes, yes, yes!" Did your mood change? When you are low on energy, I've found movement, any type of movement… getting the body in motion helps. Walk around your office building; if you're sitting, stand up and rapidly rub your hands together. Movement and breathing can change your energy level quickly.

 Step 2: Hydrate More

Dehydration is one of the most common preventable medical conditions globally, yet it affects millions. For something so common, most of us are unaware of its dangers.

CBS reports nearly 75% of us simply don't drink enough water. The institute of medicine prescribes ten cups per day. When you function daily in a chronic and persistent dehydration state, you lose focus, lose energy, lose your attention span, and increase irritability quotient. Simply drink more water.

 ### Step 3: Accept Your Emotional Level Then Redirect

Whatever you are feeling, permit yourself to feel that way. Instead of denying the reality of your feelings, acknowledge them. Consider sitting with them for a moment and then make an active decision to regroup. What's that famous quote? "You can't stop the birds from flying around your head, yet you can stop them from making a nest."

Accept, reflect, then redirect.

 ### Step 4: Take Action Towards Your Intention

Instead of listening to "I don't feel like it" now, you are in a position to take a different action. To overcome your feelings and move towards your dreams. In business and life, you state your goals and plot your course for reaching them. However, there will be many days when you don't feel like doing the work, yet go ahead and do it anyway. "Feeling like it" is not a pre-requisite.

Final thought… who's in charge, you or your feelings?

Authors note: This blog was written the week my dad passed away—a WW2 veteran, a cold war veteran, father, grandfather, and lover of the Lord. I am forever grateful for the lessons learned and the opportunities given. When I was about 10, I desperately wanted a new bike. My dad challenged me to earn half the money (thinking I never would.) I started a lawn mowing and watering business and made the cash in 60 days. He followed through on his half of the deal, and I enjoyed the bike for many years.

#WinTheDay #RIPCDJ

KEYSTONE HABITS!

**First, forget inspiration. Habit is more dependable.
Habit will sustain you whether you're inspired or not.**

~ Octavia Butler

Some habits are more important than others — they have the power to transform. Keystone habits are like throwing a pebble into the water and the ripple effect it creates. Said another way, these habits hold together all of our other habits, much like the pillars of a bridge.

Make your bed! A great book and a great video from Admiral McRaven. You see, Admiral McRaven knows that it's the little things executed consistently over time that can change our life, change our business, and change the world.

There are three characteristics of keystone habits that set them apart:

- Keystone habits make it easier to start new habits.
- Keystone habits are small enough to avoid overwhelm and build confidence.
- Keystone habits make positive behavior addictive.

When you identify your keystone habits that meet these criteria and suit your lifestyle, that is when your breakthrough begins. Need a specific example? Try taking your M.E.D.S. daily.

Consider taking your M.E.D.S. daily.
Meditation & Prayer
Exercise
Diet & Nutrition
Sleep

Charles Duhigg, author of "The Power of Habit," calls these "keystone habits." They are correlated with other good habits.

For example, studies have shown that people who regularly exercise 3 or more times a week tend to eat healthier, consume less alcohol, smoke less, be more productive at their work and sleep better than those who don't. Getting a good night of sleep isn't only for the kids. Your quality of sleep could also have a profound impact on your productivity and happiness. According to a report from the Harvard Medical School:

> *"When we are sleep deprived, our focus, attention, and vigilance drift, making it more difficult to receive information. Without adequate sleep and rest, over-worked neurons can no longer function to coordinate information properly, and we lose our ability to access previously learned information."*

Keystone habits, without them, everything seems to fall apart. But, with their support, everything seems to fall into place easier and more efficiently. Now, not all habits are positive. Think of the negative impacts that could occur in your life if you started drinking a six-pack of soda every night. Your physical health would suffer.

It's essential to recognize how one action that you do regularly can influence the larger picture. Because of this, we want to make sure that our everyday activities are leading us to become the best version of ourselves rather than hurting us in the long run. If you recognize and adopt good keystone habits, you will notice that things can improve dramatically because of one small change.

Duhigg, in his book, says, ultimately, willpower is the most critical keystone habit if you want to achieve success. Everything boils down to your self-discipline. Do you do what is right or best even though it might not be the most comfortable choice? Or do you give in to what is going to give you the most immediate satisfaction?

Change the goal or change the behavior? The choice is yours.

#WinTheDay

WILLPOWER IS OVER-RATED!

"If you have a dream, don't just sit there. Gather courage to believe that you can succeed and leave no stone unturned to make it a reality."

~ Dr. Roopleen

As a performance coach and a leader both in the military and private enterprise, I've often wondered why people say they want to change yet never do? It seems from my experience, it is our human nature to rely solely on willpower in creating change in our business and our lives: yet *what if we are thinking about it all wrong?*

In *"Willpower Doesn't Work,"* Benjamin Hardy explains that willpower is nothing more than a dangerous fad – a fad bound to lead to failure. Instead of "white-knuckling" your way to change, he suggests we need to alter our surroundings instead to support our goals. Later in this book, you will see a great outline of a few ways to "alter your surroundings" in the blog article: 7 Steps for Success in Real Estate Sales. Each of these seven steps is a practical way to alter your surroundings, create confidence, and crush your goals.

You see, working with so many of you, I know you want something bigger for yourself. I do, you do, your loved ones do.

You want to feel more in control; you want more transformation of your business. If you are relying solely on willpower, here's what I know:

> **"Willpower alone simply is not an effective approach to change."**

- Spiritually, I'd rely on my higher power than my power.
- Motivationally, I'd rely on my WHY power than my willpower.
- Behaviorally, I'd create environments of positive stress and high demand vs. staying in the status quo.

The story of John Burke. John was nominated for a Grammy for the best new album. One of the songs on this album was titled Earth Breaker. Here's the interesting thing, Earth Breaker was a song Burke didn't even know he could write or play when he started it. When he composed the music, it was beyond his current musical ability. Yet that is exactly what he wanted. He wrote a song he couldn't play and then took immediate action to practice and practice, over and over until he mastered it.

Writing a song beyond his skill level was as a "forcing function" for Burke. It created conditions with more advanced rules than he was accustomed to living. He had to GROW into the environment he created for himself. The moment Burke decides he is going to pursue a new project, he immediately decides and takes seven decisive actions.

- He decides when the project will be completed and by when it will be released.
- He works backward from the release date, mapping out all key milestones.

- He calls that day to schedule studio time.
- He pays upfront to ensure he gets his preferred studio date and time.
- Organizes his calendar and schedule to support the project.
- He passes on other opportunities that would be a distraction from his main project.
- He declares his new project publicly, creating an expectation and accountability from others.

Burke CREATES conditions that force him to succeed by taking immediate and decisive action.

So, what's holding you back?

What action can you take NOW?

If you are not in a weekly mastermind group, I encourage you to create one TODAY.

Are you role-playing with a partner the most common questions, the most common objections, and the most common tripwires daily? If not, find a partner and start TODAY.

Here is what I know *"the business world rewards action, not thought."*

If you need coaching and accountability either in a group setting or on one basis, schedule a consult today.

#WinTheDay

DON'T SETTLE FOR SAFE

I've coached many real estate professionals and entrepreneurs who just feel uninspired or flat over my career. There is one common theme:

Settling for safe!
When they were new to the business, they pushed their comfort zones, tried new and innovative things to launch a new realty business. They pushed through uncertainty to achieve a goal. Then what?

> **Certainty creeps in, settling for safe creeps in,**
> **and suddenly you feel flat.**

We all need that balance of certainty and uncertainty.
Yet, in my practice, I've seen a direct relationship between business success and uncertainty. Ironically, the more you grow, the more uncertainty surrounds you. This is because, as your business grows, everything else does too: more team members, customers, partners, competitors, and more decisions that can go right, wrong, or indifferent.

Because there is no certainty about what will happen during a time of change, many leaders either try to control events or simply shut down. Both can be problematic and lead you to sub-optimal results.

I've observed that my most thriving associates deal with change and uncertainty by focusing on daily progress - which provides comfort and clarity - allowing them to embrace and create uncertainty.

How? Consider these four steps:

Winning the day
You can embrace uncertainty with healthy daily habits like taking your M.E.D.S. Meditate, exercise, diet (nutrition), and sleep.

Give the status quo a jab, jab, hook
The associates I've worked with that struggle have convinced themselves that their status quo is precisely what they deserve. And they go about and base their identities around that belief. I've observed that my associates live where they have attached their identity. The good news? We have the power to choose the meaning we attach to anything. Make a compelling choice and give the status quo a jab, jab, hook

Connecting to a compelling vision and reason
We all solve problems for a profit. What does your ideal day, week, and month look like? It's proven, you will face hurdles when embracing uncertainty, and it is the reason "why" that will push you through to the other side. What matters most is that your reasons resonate with you deeply, not just superficially.

Burn the boats
In 1519, Captain Hernán Cortés landed in Veracruz to begin his conquest. Upon arriving, he gave an order to his troops to

burn the ships in which they arrived. In essence, he gave them no other option but to succeed at the goal of conquering.

Burn the boats is a concept where you leave no other option for yourself in context to something you would like to achieve.

So, there you have it embracing uncertainty. Win the day; give the status quo a jab, jab, hook; connect to a compelling reason and burn the boats!

#WinTheDay

THE POWER OF CRISIS TO TRANSFORM

Not sure about you; for me, it is overwhelming to see how the world has come together in this crisis of COVID-19. As McChesney, Covey, and Huling wrote so well in the "4 Disciplines of Execution," when you have "singularity of focus," the trivial gets minimized.

Yet, for me, it's also a paradox, the dichotomy of our lives right now as we push forward in adapting to new work routines, new ways of connecting, and new ways of contributing to our communities. At the same time, we watch first responders, doctors, nurses, and even the local grocery store staff pour their hearts each day into serving others. It's been inspiring to see the greatness in humanity.

This week at JPAR, we started a free series called the 8 AM club. The intention was to help our associates, staff, and business partners adapt to new routines, new ways of working, and delivering empowering messages to help adapt during this time of transition.

On Monday, **Seth Denson** shared the power of a solid foundation. "Did You Build It Right?"

Tuesday, **Tanya Waymire** shared "How You Choose To Show Up Is Everything."

Wednesday, **Jose Ruiz** shared the science of "Being Intentional."

Thursday, **Germaine Gaspard** shared a powerful message about: "Know This: What You Are Becoming Is What You Are Doing."

Friday, we capped off the week with **Sylvia Marusk**, who shared: "Stress - the Silent Killer."

The series is just one step we are taking to ensure our JPAR associates, staff, and partners don't just survive - they thrive.

Next week's theme? How to deal with things when they go out of control.

> **If you don't like it, change it.**
> **If you can't change it, change the way you think about it!**

It seems we are all spending a lot more time sharing, talking, and communicating on video platforms and social media. This virus event will change us in ways we've never imagined. Yet here's what I know – we are all in it together.

As I was thinking, just a few weeks ago, most of us would say, "we don't have the time!" Time is currency. And now we have all the time in the world. What will you do with it?

Here are a few action items to consider:

Throw out the OLD rules

One of my favorite movies - Apollo 13 - has a scene where ground control is calling up a new procedure for the astronauts. "Aquarius, this is Houston; we'd like you to rip the cover off your flight plan!"

Your 2020 business plan just changed, and I'd like you to rip the virtual cover off your plan and write a new procedure.

At JPAR, we have written a 21-question digital business review, now is the time to dig into that review and rewrite the plan.

First, make sure your database is ready to support you and your growth. My surveys show 50% still work off sticky notes and spreadsheets... now is the time to get organized.

Second, find a market that fits your selling style. Then, find an area ready for your focus. Hyperlocal expertise will never be more important. Be a specialist, not a generalist.

Third, leverage video. A bad video is better than no video. Consistency and value are key.

Fourth, social media. Be helpful. It does not need to all be about business.

Fifth, now is not the time for marketing as usual.
- Leverage the free resources at KCM and NAR. Consider starting a FB group for your neighbors, moms' groups, and guys.
- Host a weekly happy hour or weekly virtual meetups
- Send texts, calls, or ten handwritten notes a day – thinking of you, how about you doing, is there anything I can do to support you?

- Pause the door-knocking & flyer drop-offs
- Use FB groups as a way to be helpful, not to sell yourself
- Turn off or update any automation the send out nonrelevant content

BUILD A SOLID ROUTINE

One size does not fit all! You're probably tired of hearing the same old line... do these four things in the morning. The truth is my routine may or may not work for you.

There have been a lot of successful people over the centuries of human history. And if you look at just a few of them, they certainly don't do the same things. But what they do have in common are daily routines, something that they do day in and day out, without fail.

The key is finding the routine that works for you.

In his book, "The Miracle Morning," Hal Elrod outlines the science, system, and secrets of a powerful routine, even if you are not a morning person! One of the most powerful concepts I learned from Hal is to "set your intentions before bed!"

BUILD COMMUNITY

You know that feeling of connection when shared goals and interests bind us together? There has never been a greater need for connection, for services, for innovative solutions during this time.

Wants and needs are all around you. We know the problem; can you provide the solution for your sphere of influence?

One example is a JPAR agent featuring a virtual interview each day on Facebook with a local business owner with a drive-through and delivery of drop-off services.

RELY ON EXPERTS TO STRENGTHEN YOUR VOICE

Separating charged emotions from facts and data is an essential skill these days. One of the best ways to amplify expertise and convey calm is to leverage other voices of authority.

One of the best is my good friend Steve Harney, Founder of Keeping Current Matters and, of course, our National Association Of REALTORS®.

And of course, we can all review reliable information from national sources such as the Center for Disease Control (CDC)

PASSION OVER PERSUASION

Do you find yourself getting mired in detail of this crisis? It is not uncommon – as I recommend above - to surround ourselves with technical experts and forget the power of human nature.

Crises are not solved with reason and data alone. We must never forget we are first and foremost humans with emotions. We have families and lives outside of deeply important work. When we lead with empathy, we demonstrate dedication and compassion for those we serve.

There you have it. Time is currency. And now that we all have some extra time, what will you do with it?

Throw out the old rules; build a new solid routine; rely on the experts to strengthen your voice and remember the most: your strategy matters and your passion rules!

#WinTheDay

THE 90 DAY HUSTLE

I love the December holiday season - it's a time of reflection and redirection - a time where everyone is just a little bit kinder, gentle, and more giving. As we enter the last few days of the year, I trust your kindness will be known to all.

Your business and marketing plans are ready... you are reflecting on what worked, what didn't, and the adjustments you will make in the New Year.

Here is what I know from working with agents, teams, and brokerage business plans all over the world:

6 BUSINESS PLAN MISTAKES YOU CAN AVOID

➲**One** – Most of us are not thinking BIG enough; if your plan is too comfortable, it's probably too small. Everyone reading this – and has the desire – can DOUBLE their business next year.

➲**Two** – Not being very clear on where the business is coming from today and how you will continue or expand that AND the few TESTS you will do each quarter of the year to create new business sources.

⟳**Three** – Doing more of the same thing and expecting a different result. What is working? What is not working? What do you need to do MORE of? What do you need to do LESS of?

⟳**Four** – Not breaking down the details into a DAILY ACTION

⟳**Five** – Not having the leading and lagging indicators UP and VISUAL… an "in your face" reminder. Like a scoreboard at a sporting event. The #1 KPI to measure is the number of new appointments created each day.

⟳**Six** – Not being clear on the benefits – the why – and what happens when you do or don't achieve the outcome.

Bonus mistake to avoid, not breaking out your marketing execution into a separate and specific plan with the actions, expected result, costs, and a content calendar. This would include a weekly or monthly social media content calendar.

CREATING A 90-DAY HUSTLE

A 90-day hustle point is that it stops you from focusing on all your goals for the year. Instead, the 90-day hustle allows you to take your plans for the year and then break them down into 90-day stretches, 30-day stretches, 2-week sprints, and y DAILY ACTIVITIES.

 STEP 1: Review your goals

Studies show your goals should be no more than 3 (major ones) at any one time, and then you'll break those down into all the steps needed to achieve them… those become part of your 90-day stretches.

Take your business & marketing plan, look at your primary goals, and then think about how you will break them down into smaller chunks, so achieving them is just a little easier.

This would be an excellent time to review the art & science of goal setting located in the bonus section of this book

STEP 2: Review your business & marketing plan

Make sure your business plan includes a specific marketing plan. The particular marketing you will do... the expected outcome of that marketing, the cost and the days, dates, and time it will be consistently executed.

Check that your plans are consistent with your goals and avoid the six biggest mistakes outlined earlier.

STEP 3: Put it all together into a 90-day hustle!

Once you've reviewed your goals and your strategic plan, think about the next three months and what you want to focus on to achieve your 2-3 main overarching goals.

Pick 1-3 steps to focus on for the next 90 days. Don't try to do it all. Less is MORE. Research shows you shouldn't be doing any more than three main things over the next 90 days. Less is more and proven.

Break these down further into daily, weekly, and 30-day stretches. Consider using an APP like PRODUCTIVITY to get accountability on everyday actions.

Include all the nitty-gritty details in your 90-day hustle. Work backward... start with your overall goal for the next 90 days and break this down into all the steps you need to take to achieve it. Don't forget to schedule your downtime, family time, charity obligations, then SCHEDULE IT in your calendar and reminder APP with alerts or alarms. There you have it, six checkpoints to validate your business plan and a format for a 90-day hustle.

I'm often asked, Mark, what should I add to my business? Consider this: always be testing... pick one promising idea (grove it) and then considering adding another promising idea every 90 days.

Always keep in mind that research shows 70% of consumers **FIND** you from a friend, family member, referral, or prior business relationship. And 70% **CHOOSE** you based on your reputation, trustworthiness, and results. These **FACTS** have significant implications for your marketing.

Have you considered testing:
- Drone photography creates trust with consumers
- Annotated virtual tours – notes from you and the seller – create trust with consumers
- A virtual walkthrough of the home with you narrating is valued MORE by consumers
- A consistent process to re-working previous leads from ALL sources like verse.io
- Creating a goal – and tracking it – like two referrals or more per year from all past clients and everyone, you know?
- More Personalization in everything you do? (We are in a relationship business, yes?!)
- More use of VIDEO? (Community and local business highlights)

- Are you building your "out of market" referral network? Who is moving into your area from out of state or across the state?
- Are you inviting curious neighbors to virtual open houses?
- Online lead generation – dark posts – that YOU control – FB, Google?
- Is this the year to wear a name badge or other branded swag?
- Leveraging or building your consumer REVIEWS?
- Are you becoming the HUB of ALL things in your community – for your sphere – for all items in your area?

So, what is YOUR 90-day hustle going to look like? And who is holding you accountable?

#WinTheDay

6 CHARACTERISTICS OF SUCCESS

"Thoughts Lead To Purpose; Purpose Drives Action; Action Form Habits; Habits Create Character; Character Defines Destiny."

~Tyron Edwards

Success comes in many ways and forms. Gandhi was successful in leading India into independence from the British. Mother Teresa was successful, giving hope to the poorest of the poor. Warren Buffett is successful in investing and building long-term business ventures.

Recently I ran across an article that outlined over 20 years of research on success. The study found certain core activities, beliefs, and attitudes shared by those who succeed.

The basic formula:
- Get clear about what you do want.
- Get clear about what you don't want.
- Visualize and feel the outcome.
- Clear your mind of self-limiting beliefs.
- Take action.

The six most typical characteristics:
1. **Resilience** – the ability to keep getting up despite being knocked down.

2. **Self-control** – the ability to subdue one's impulses, emotions, and behaviors to achieve longer-term goals.

3. **Emotional awareness** – Emotional awareness is the ability to recognize your own emotions and those of others.

4. **Creativity** – the ability to perceive the world in new ways using two processes: thinking and producing.

5. **Optimism** – does not take failure personally but keeps on trying until he succeeds and expects positive outcomes

6. **Sociability**

So, where do you stand?

Once your beliefs and actions are aligned, there are no limits.

#WinTheDay

3 STEPS TO MASTERY

"The most beautiful form of mastery is the art of letting go."

~ Claudia Gray

Who doesn't want to be a better agent, better team leader, a better entrepreneur? If there is one concept that can lead to more robust performance with immediate impact… this is it:

It's difficult to control our thoughts and feelings, yet we have total control of our actions.

Here's what I know:
- **Actions change attitudes**
- **Motions change emotions**
- **Movement changes moods**

Think about it. It is much easier to act yourself into a particular way of feeling than to feel your way into a specific way of acting. This may sound counter-intuitive, yet research repeatedly has proven the shortest, most reliable way to change how you're feeling is to change what you're doing. When you feel bad, don't wait to feel good to do what you love. Start doing what you love.

My friend and business coach, Tom Ferry, and life coach Tony Robbins both have a beautiful way of describing the steps to mastery in just about anything:

- **MINDSET, MODELS & MARKETING.** Model something or someone who's already achieved what you want. You can compress years into days by having the right model. I call it the 3 M's of success: mindset, models, and marketing.

- **TOTAL IMMERSION.** You have to immerse yourself in the thing you are trying to master.

- **SPACED REPETITION.** You need repetition. It is only by repetition that you can condition yourself properly and one day become a master at something. This is like our real estate playbook – designed to create four new transactions – inside your 5-week course and our annual September March To Greatness campaign.

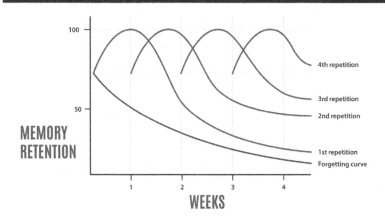

FORGETTING CURVE FOR NEWLY LEARNED INFORMATION

My acquaintance Dr. Rob Gilbert says it another way.

"If you want to be a champion, then the work is no problem. When your commitment is greater than your feelings, you'll master whatever you desire."

Who is in charge, you or your feelings?

If you want to learn about mastery, I recommend George Leonard's book called: Mastery.

#WinTheDay

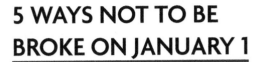

5 WAYS NOT TO BE BROKE ON JANUARY 1

"For last year's words belong to last year's language And next year's words await another voice."

~ T.S. Eliot, Four Quartets

Typically, I wrote this blog about 90 days out from the New Year. And I ask this one question:

What will your bank account look like on January 1?

Is it your desire to have a more significant bank account or a smaller one? Whatever your goal is, NOW is the time to make that happen.

The next 90 days will be critical for setting yourself up for a strong close and a fast start to the new year. What you do in the next few days and weeks will determine your bank account's size on January 1 and your momentum for the first quarter of the following year.

CHALLENGE 1: What would happen to your business if, for the next 75 working days, you made one new appointment each day?

Let's face there are two types of agents today: hobbyists and CEO's. This article is not for hobbyists, those part-time agents who dabble. Those of you that run your business like a business, those of you who know your daily number, and understand what it takes to generate one sale, then this article is for you.

CHALLENGE 2: Get clear about the next 90 days:

- Write down the number of sales you've made so far this year.
- Write down the source of those sales.
- How many listings will you earn between now and the end of the year?
- How many additional families or investors do you want to serve between now and the end of the year?
- How many contacts do you need to make to drive that number?
- One rule of thumb is 40 contacts to 1 sale.
- Who are they, and how will you go about connecting with them?
- What systems do you have in place to create the result you desire?

After completing the quick exercise above, here are five actions you can take so you're not broke on January 1:

- **Decide Now.** Decide now how many days you will work, how many days you will be off, and how many "flex days" you'll have between now and the end of the year. Decide what direct response marketing campaigns you will run. For example, if you will create an investor campaign to take advantage of year-end investment buyers.

- **Up your CRM game. There is no excuse for not having your CRM updated and working for you. It takes discipline,** yet once you realize your CRM is the engine that drives your train, that task becomes less negotiable.

- **Delegate.** Is it time to find some help? An office or virtual assistant. Your highest and best use is *prospecting; lead generation; going on appointments, and negotiating contracts.* Everything else automate, delegate, or eliminate. Scared? Get resourceful; many new agents I know share a fractional assistant to split cost yet keep them fully employed.

- **Diversify your lead generation sources. Too many struggling agents rely on ONE, maybe TWO lead sources. FOUR sources of business – split between influence strategies and control strategies – provides diversity and stability to your real estate practice.**

- Your database and sphere – a daily process of at least five contacts
- Virtual Open houses – 1x per week
- Geographic targeting – 2 campaigns per month
- Online leads

Note, don't add four sources all at once. Start with one new source, get it working and stable, then add another until you reach four sources.

- Target Market Clarity? Any market rewards the hyperlocal expert. Are you an expert in a community? Are you an expert in a profession like Nurses, FBI agents, CPA's? It's probably time to get hyperlocal and specialize.

So, I'll leave you today with three final things to consider:

1. Knowing what you know now, what immediate adjustments do you need to make?

2. Cash is king. Are you building your cash reserves? Are you reducing bad debt? Investing in marketing?

3. Have you started a small weekly accountability group with like-minded, goal-oriented CEO's like yourself? If not, what's holding you back?

#WinTheDay

THE TOP 1%

R udy is a true story about persistence, tenacity, grit, and football. A football game isn't won on the field. The game is won in the days, weeks, and even months leading up to the actual game. The game is won in preparation. Watching films of previous games, memorizing plays, hitting the gym, eating correctly, and even getting enough sleep.

Professional real estate sales is no different.
I've been spending some time with our top 1% documenting what they do. Curious?

Here are the top six things our top 1% do consistently:

- They do their research.
- They're genuinely interested in and understand others' personality style.
- They're prepared for anything.
- They leave their ego in the car.
- They are a master of managing expectations.
- The debrief and learn from every situation.

RESEARCH
We know from the National Association of REALTORS® that 63% of consumers find us through a referral from a friend or

a past business relationship. And 68% of consumers choose us based on our perceived trustworthiness, experience, and reputation.

Top producers know these numbers and invest their time, energy, and effort into where the business is most likely to be generated.

GENUINE INTEREST

What we have observed from top producers to those struggling is glaring. Top producers genuinely care about the relationship while those struggling care about making a buck.

We use a unique system called B.A.N.K. to pinpoint anyone's personality in nanoseconds. It's fun, engaging, and creates instant rapport. Crack your code now; it's easy: www.jparcode. com This high emotional intelligence approach leverages the best assessment tools, high-energy training, and cutting-edge technology to maximize results.

LEAVE NOTHING TO CHANCE

Our top performers rehearse or role-play frequently; many do this every day! Here are some tips I picked up:

- Make a list of every question, concern, or objection that your prospect might bring up. Create a list of everything that could go wrong.
- Develop a clear, logical, and persuasive response to every possible question, concern, and objection.
- Think of how you can get ahead of these circumstances by using stories and anecdotes, case studies and testimonials, statistics, and facts.

- Have your information, ideas, and documentation well organized so you can reference the appropriate notes and materials at any time.

EGO

Gary Vaynerchuk put it well: "When you care more about the other person than you care about hitting your quota - when you make that shift - you go into the Jedi-ness of becoming a great salesperson."

The professional real estate salesperson with a massive ego can easily mistake refusal with rejection. When you make this mistake, it's all too easy to take it personally. The truth? Far more people will say no than say yes.

So, how do you deal with this?

Our top 1% have learned not to internalize rejection. Top performers exert power over their emotions and know this is a critical skill to master.

MANAGING EXPECTATIONS

As the Chief Executive of a large organization, I get the problems that others have not solved. And literally, I've been tracking these, and guess what - they all have a common root. Uneven expectations!

Many things have to happen, often in a specific sequence, before a transaction closes. Do you know what these things are? Do you know where you're at in the process with each client, prospect, and partner?

1. Seek to understand what has come before each step
2. Don't assume everyone knows what will happen next
3. Anticipate needs before others
4. Communicate constantly and clearly
5. Under-promise and over-deliver

DEBRIEF

Debriefing is a structured learning process designed to evolve plans while they're being executed continuously. It originated in the military to learn quickly in rapidly changing situations and address mistakes or changes in the field. I fact, I shared this document with my team - *glad to be here* - after the Blue Angels flew over Dallas.

In business, debriefing has been widely documented as critical to accelerating projects, innovating novel approaches, and hitting challenging objectives. It also brings a team together, strengthens relationships, and fosters team learning.

Our top producers have this concept mastered and execute this discipline more often than others. As such, these high performing teams are more tight-knit than those who don't.

The game is won or lost way before you step on the playing field. So, before you play in sales again, do your research, be genuinely interested in others, be prepared for anything, leave your ego in the car, and become a master of managing expectations. Finally - just like the Blue Angels - debrief and learn from every situation.

#WinTheDay

DECISION TIME

"Whenever you see a successful business, someone once made a courageous decision."

~ Peter F. Drucker

To delay is to make the right decision even harder eventually.

"Indecision is a decision."

Because not deciding is a choice, decisions are made whether we make them or not.

Bottom line: time is our enemy, and time ALWAYS wins unless action is taken. What we are not changing, we are choosing.

What will you take action on TODAY?

#WinTheDay

GOAL MAGIC

"Shoot for the moon. Even if you miss, you'll land among the stars."

~ **Les Brown**

O ne of my coaches from several years ago helped me learn a valuable lesson:

"The fastest way to change how you feel is to change how you THINK!"

When you change the way you look at things, the things you look at change. When you change the way, you think it changes how you feel. When you change the way, you feel it changes the way you act. And when you act more consistently towards your goals, magic happens.

What thinking pattern do you need to interrupt today?

#WinTheDay

WHAT MATTERS MOST: THE MOST URGENT OR THE MOST IMPORTANT?

"The bad news is time flies. The good news is you're the pilot."

~ Michael Altshuler

If you are like me, you face the challenge each day of choosing urgent and important matters. I've been struggling with this balance lately and wanted to re-ground myself in those things I know are important, helpful, and useful in focusing on those activities that make a real difference.

Every expert I've asked agrees – if you let urgent matters consume your time, you'll never get to those important projects, activities, or tasks. In many cases, those important projects, activities, and tasks are the ones that generate the most revenue, creates the most satisfied clients, or help you be more productive in delivering an exceptional consumer experience. The word project here does not necessarily mean a specific project. It could be a task or activity. For example, cultivating relationships with clients, vendors, or coworkers, acknowledging a job well done, taking time to improve a skill, or focus on your health by exercising, are all important but not urgent activities.

Stephen Covey recorded an exercise with rocks of different sizes (small, medium, and large rocks) and a glass pitcher. Students see all the rocks in the container, and the instructor empties the container and then has a student try and get all the rocks back in the pitcher. Most, if not all, the students failed to get all the rocks back in – they typically start by placing all the small rocks in the pitcher and then trying to stuff the remaining large rocks into the pitcher. The instructor steps in, place the big rocks in the pitcher first, and then all the little rocks fall into place, and they all fit!

	Urgent		Not Urgent	
	Quad I		**Quad II**	
Important	Activities • Crisis • Pressing Problems • Deadline Driven	Results • Stress • Burn-out • Crisis management • Always putting out fires	Activities • Prevention, capability improvement • Relationship building • Recognizing new opportunities • Planning, recreation	Results • Vision, perspective • Balance • Discipline • Control • Few crisis
	Quad III		**Quad IV**	
Not Important	Activities • Interruptions, some callers • Some email, some reports • Some meetings • Proximate, pressing matters • Popular activities	Results • Short term focus • Crisis management • Reputation – chameleon character • See goals/ plans as worthless • Feel victimized, out of control • Shallow or broken relationships	Activities • Trivia, busy work • Some email • Personal social media • Some phone calls • Time wasters • Pleasant activities	Results • Total irresponsibility • Fired from jobs • Dependent on others or institutions for basics

Few of us have the luxury of focusing on just the urgent or just the important; to be successful, you must manage the important and the urgent. How can you handle both? Keep the big picture priorities in front of you at all times. Do you have a "top 5" list? What are the outcomes you what to achieve? Keeping the big picture close to you makes it easier to get back on track after an "urgent" distraction is handled.

Turn your email off and only focus on email during specific times during the day. Schedule your important items as actual appointments – schedule specific times to focus on your most important projects when urgent matters don't normally occur. The phrase, "How do you eat an elephant? One bite at a time" comes to mind.

Urgent matters get in the way, so plan for it! There are certain things in our business that we can plan on happening. These urgent matters draw you away from your important priorities. Schedule these interruptions as part of your daily routine.

Before you tackle an urgent matter, ask yourself how important it is to do "right now." Can it wait? Can someone else handle this? Is it an excuse to get off task and avoid the more challenging work of the important project list?

What you measure, you can manage. Here is a proposed action plan to help you see your pattern. This week, keep a journal and take note of the following:

1. What task or project you are working on?
2. How much time are you devoting to this task?
3. Why are you doing this task?

At the end of each day, write a "U" for urgent or "I" for important next to each entry. How do these activities relate to your big picture and overall priorities?

After The Week Is Over, Read Through Your Journal And Cover These 7 Areas:

1. How many U's and I's, did you have?
2. Are you closer to achieving your big picture or farther away?

3. How many U's could have been bypassed or delegated to others?
4. How does the U's interfere with your I's?
5. If your number of I's is low, what got in the way?
6. How can you better manage or cut out some of these U's?
7. Are you avoiding your I's?

If urgent items keep getting in the way, stop the madness. Talk to a trusted advisor, business coach, or counselor and clarify some strategies for staying focused on the important while handling the urgent.

PRODUCTIVITY AND TIME

"You get to decide where your time goes. You can either spend it moving forward, or you can spend it putting out fires. You decide. And if you don't decide, others will decide for you."

~ Tony Morgan

I've met a few people who simply accomplish more in 24 hours than anyone else in my career.

When asked about their "secret," there is a trend. Most say, "I take 5 minutes at the end of every hour to evaluate how the previous 55 minutes went. Were they productive? Were they profitable? Was it the highest and best use of my time? Whatever they discovered that was negative to any of the three questions, they did a pivot and got back on track doing the things that matter. From there, they develop a personal operating philosophy for "time optimization."

THERE ARE THREE RULES:

Rule #1: Measure your hourly rate. Over the last several months, how many hours did you work, and how much did you make per hour? *Bonus: use the worksheet at the back of this book.*

Rule #2: Measure where you are losing revenue. What tasks are you involved in that isn't earning you top dollar? What can be delegated, automated, or eliminated? What can you do more efficiently?

Rule #3: Determine how much more you can make. If you deconstruct your time use, you can reallocate your time freed up to more profitable activities over time.

#WinTheDay

YOUR MINDSET MATTERS...
MORE THAN YOU THINK

Success is not an accident; success is a choice.

~ Stephen Curry

I recently ran across a blog from Los Silva about how he and others did not merely double their business; they 10X'd their business. Los is the Co-Founder & CEO of The Collective, one of the world's top fitness publishing companies with over 250,000 customers all over the world. He also runs SVG media, a training and education company that helps entrepreneurs scale past their limits.

What does this have to do with real estate and your real estate practices? Plenty, your mindset matters, and that's the key focus for today's repost of his blog.

Here are five strategies from Los Silva for getting yourself into the 10x mindset today:

1. **Forget self-discipline. Focus on your habits.** Remember that book, The Seven Habits of Highly Effective People? It's not lying to you—effective people have effective habits, and the opposite is also true. You need to be aware of your habits.

Ask yourself which are going to help you grow ten times and which are holding you back. It's time to start making changes like learning to say no to things that don't help you achieve your goals and adequately caring for your physical and mental health. Most importantly, you've got to learn to let go of the control complex that's preventing you from delegating critical aspects of your business to capable employees and coworkers while you focus on growth. When you work on ditching the bad habits and cultivating the good, you allow your perspective to shift from scarcity toward a potential future where anything is possible.

2. **Clean up your mindset.** Everyone makes mistakes, and mistakes make a mess. By mess, we mean issues that aren't yet resolved in your mind and are still floating around in the gray muck of unconsciousness, eating up your mental RAM. Essentially, a mess feels obligated to something or someone that you no longer commit to. For many entrepreneurs, this means getting out of the personal office and into a conference room, café, bar, or anywhere else that doesn't carry the massive amount of mental baggage lying around wherever you call home. By getting away from the messes—and slowly working to remove them—you will get much more productivity from your work and quality from your life. It takes a lot of energy to clear these out, but it's crucial to do so. You can then move forward and work to prevent future messes.

3. **Strengthen your relationships** by focusing on the value you're providing. If you have a myopic focus on sales, you're missing out on vital information about your customers and clientele. Instead of spending all of your time trying to get money coming in, focus on providing ten times the value to

your customers and clients. You'll quickly become one of their favorite people, and that's the time to ask brave questions: Do you know their pain points? Their dreams and goals? Their strengths and capabilities? If you genuinely listen to them, you have the opportunity to form long-lasting, incredibly profitable, and valuable relationships with them that will allow you to grow at a rate beyond your—and your competition's—wildest dreams.

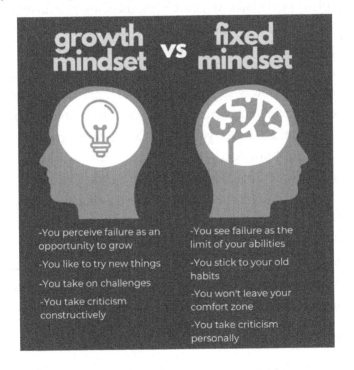

growth mindset vs fixed mindset

-You perceive failure as an opportunity to grow

-You like to try new things

-You take on challenges

-You take criticism constructively

-You see failure as the limit of your abilities

-You stick to your old habits

-You won't leave your comfort zone

-You take criticism personally

4. **Conquer setbacks by focusing on results**. It's a good thing for leaders to be able to foresee obstacles that could arise. It's a bad thing if leaders become afraid or overwhelmed by the potential for things to go wrong. Be honest about obstacles, take them one-by-one, and approach them with a results-focused strategy that draws on the capabilities of your

entire team to multiply your abilities. Once you get in the habit of approaching obstacles not as something to be afraid of but as something that's a natural part of goal-achieving, you can start extending what you've learned to your customers and clientele. You can take your relationship past mere financial transactions to a place of trust and mutual effort.

5. **Increase everyone's confidence by focusing on capability.** In the United States Marine Corps, there are two sayings they teach you in boot camp: "Fake it until you make it," and, "Confidence is 90% of all effort." That is, even if you don't know what you're doing, have the confidence to try it anyway! You never know what you're capable of until you try—or until a drill instructor is screaming at you and spraying tobacco-tinged spittle all over your face. Confidence isn't something people are born with—it's something that's worked on and built up over time. Think of it as a muscle that needs to be exercised. One way to exercise it is to continually review your achievements and use them to gain insight into how you can tweak your future efforts. Another way is to identify your excellent capabilities—the one or two that you have that you're truly a genius at—and then identify those same unique capabilities in your team. Ask yourself—and them—what it would look like if this capability grew by ten times.

Nothing is standing in the way of you and a business that's ten times larger, ten times more effective, and ten times more profitable. Get the mindset, make the connection, apply the method, and watch the vehicle for your passions, goals, and dreams take off.

#WinTheDay

YOUR BUSINESS IS LIKE A ROWING TEAM

"A coach is someone who always makes you do what you don't want to do so you can be who you've always wanted to be."

~ Tom Landry

This week, I spent some time in our Austin, Texas market, where one of our REALTOR® **team leaders is a "coxswain" and a rowing coach.** He told me a story about a new rower placed on a boat with eight others... he noticed she appeared to be working very hard and sweating profusely. Yet, her technique was so off it wasn't helping the team.

Can you relate to a time where you've been working hard and not getting the result you intended?

A rowing team – and your business – need more than just quality, skilled resources. You also need all your resources in the right seats, doing the right things.

Here's the thing I learned about rowing: in an eight-person boat, each rower has one oar—four on port and four on starboard. If one side pulls harder than the other side, the boat turns. If one side's oars are raised higher than the other side, the boat tips. To find the set and create a swing, everyone must work together to balance the boat and have exact timing. Your hands must be at exactly the right height as you slide up to the catch. Every oar has to drop into the water at the exact same time. Everyone needs to pull at equal pressure. All the blades need to come out of the water and release in unison. Any deviation disrupts the boat.

So, what can we learn?

First, have a clear direction, but an easy hand on the steering
The "coxswain" job is to keep the boat on course and steer the straightest line possible. Steering too much means zig-zagging over the course and rowing far more than 2,000 meters, which adds to the time. The trick is to keep the end in sight and steer to a center point far down course, not trying to keep coming back to the center every stroke. To do this, the coxswain calls out increased pressure for a few strokes on one side of the boat or the other to correct the course rather than use the rudder, which slows down the boat.

Learning: High-performance teams always keep the end in sight and know the ultimate objectives of their work. Without a clear picture of the goal, teams thrash with process and fail to achieve proper alignment in their activities. Going in the wrong direction as fast as you can doesn't get you any closer to the finish.

Second, it's not how hard you work; it's how hard you work together
It turns out that pulling as hard as you can without pulling together actually slows the boat down. Imbalanced power will

veer the boat one direction and throw off the catch and release timing. Uncontrolled straining at the oar can tip your weight left or right and toss the boat side to side. A successful team pulls in perfect balance and with perfect timing.

Learning: Successful teams know that performance is a function of collaboration and coordination, not a sum of individual effort. Knowing how your contribution affects the outcome and staying highly aware of what others are doing while staying in sync is critical to delivering results. Reacting quickly, deliberately and in a coordinated fashion allows teams to adapt to changes, handle new information, and stay on target.

Make it a decisive week.

#WinTheDay

WOULD YOU CHOOSE UNPLEASANT TRUTHS OR COMFORTING LIES?

E very picture tells a story, and that's true of today's blog post photo. Take a look… that image just may have hit home for you as it did for me.

I have few regrets… yet recently, I happened to be in a business meeting where we moved the chess prices around the board however did not address the real underlying issue. Instead, I chose the path of least resistance… the path of comfort instead of the harder truth. The conflict was avoided, yet so was the real growth opportunity. Can you relate to a similar situation in your business or life?

While comforting lies can be, well, comforting, they won't help us get through a challenging situation in a way that serves our mutual best interests. Comforting lies won't help you grow. So, if your desire is to be the best version of you, switch the line you're in. Move from the easy line of comfort to the more challenging line. The unpleasant truth will equip you with the feedback to make the best next step. The next best course of action given your circumstances, desires, and dreams.

As a mentor, coach, and consultant, here's what I know:

> *"a coach is someone who tells you what you don't want to hear, who has you see what you don't want to see, so you can be who you have always known you could be."*

Let's be that person this week for all the people we influence.

#WinTheDay

LIFE ON THE WIRE

This past week, the conversation around my watercooler has been work-life balance. It reminded me of my acquaintance, author, and coach, Todd Duncan. He challenges the status quo in his book "Life On The Wire. Rejecting how-to formulas claiming to know the perfect balance between work and life, he argues that such a holy grail does not exist. Instead, he offers readers a solution of purposeful imbalance: the process of purposefully leaning toward work without sacrificing life and intentionally leaning toward a life without damaging your career. Like the art of tightrope walking, the key to not falling is taking things one step at a time.

For me, work-life balance can seem like an impossible feat. Technology makes entrepreneurs like us accessible around the clock. 94% of entrepreneurs reported working more than 50 hours per week, and half said they worked more than 65 hours per week.

Experts agree: the compounding stress from the never-ending workday is damaging. It can hurt relationships, health, and overall happiness.

I'm personally on a massive "unsubscribe" campaign this week. Think about it - 5 Quintillion bytes of data are created every day. Every two days, we create as much information that has been created since the dawn of civilization up until 2003. So consider this.

The silent epidemic: information overload. A symptom of our addiction to novelty - like the ping of a new notification - a trigger to not focus on what's important and chase a distraction.

Choices that drive focus:
Relevance
Filtering
Rejecting (the art of saying no)
Delegate, automate, or eliminate

So, what can we do about this phenomenon?

Consider this seven-step plan:

1. Letting GO of perfectionism and make a decision!
   a. Done is better than perfect
   b. A plan executed NOW better than a strategy thought about for months
2. Unplug – plan it in your calendar
3. Exercise and Prayer
4. Limit time-wasting activities and people
5. Change it up... are you in a rut?
6. Start small build new routines
7. Stay intentional
   a. Overwhelmed? Stuck? Paralyzed?
   b. Give yourself permission to let go and only focus on what you need now.

c. If you are in a situation where you feel overwhelmed and don't know what course to take, "just do the next right thing."

With this seven-step plan, you can move from being stuck to being inspired.

Whose is ALL in?

#WinTheDay

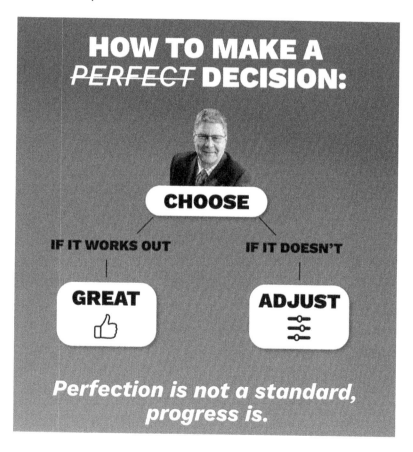

ADDICTED TO ADDICTIONS!

Believe you can, and you're halfway there.

~ Theodore Roosevelt

So, what gets in your way?

THE FOUR ADDICTIONS:
Tom Ferry, my friend, and mentor discovered and wrote about in his book "Life By Design" four addictions that destroy more dreams, more hopes, and more lives than alcohol, drugs, food, gambling, or sex combined.

You and I typically think of addictions as the effects of four much larger causes that are the root cause. Here is what Tom wrote:

The Addiction to opinions of other people. Some people are addicted to what others think about us and how others' views of the world affect us.

The Addiction to drama. Some people are drawn to and consumed by any event or situation that occupies their thoughts and fills their minds with negativity, which often brings attention to them in unproductive ways.

The Addiction to the past. These people have an unhealthy attachment to events or situations that have occurred in the past. They are stuck in how things used to be.

The Addiction to worry. This addiction is comprised of all the negative and self-defeating thoughts that make us anxious, disturbed, upset, and stressed, that hold us back in life. Of which, most of all, never come true.

Tom shared some advice he learned from the great Mike Vance to create a path out of these addictions. Five action-provoking and life-altering questions to help me envision what's possible. The road less traveled.

The 5 Killer Questions!
- What are your God-given talents?
- Why are you here — what is your purpose?
- How do you want to show up for others — what are your values?
- Five years from now, how is the world experiencing you?
- Who would you already be if you were already there?

You know I once had the opportunity to complete a workout with Jillian Michaels, America's personal trainer. I was able to ask her what was one of the factors that lead to her breakthrough… she said:

"Mark, once I figured out the opinions of other people, don't pay my bills, that's when my breakthrough began!"

Said another way, my acquaintance Dr. Daniel Amen, "the brain doctor, as I call him, challenges us to remember the 18-40-60 Rule.

- At 18, you worry about what others think about you.
- At 40, you don't care what others think about you.
- At 60, you realize no one has been thinking about you at all.

People think about themselves, not you.

So true!

As we wrap up today's, blog understanding "cause and effect" make us stronger.

Consider this: we know the cause is an action that makes something else (the effect) happen. So, what happens when:

You become more intentional?
When you surround yourself with ambitious people?
When you keep giving fuel to the fire of your ambition?

How do you keep your motivation alive?

#WinTheDay

CAN YOU HAVE IT ALL?

"All our dreams can come true if we have the courage to pursue them."

~ Walt Disney

In one of our major markets, recently our company learned it was performing nearly four times better than the market average. That's a big win amid a global pandemic.

That got me to thinking how did our real estate sales associates do it? What is in our culture that makes this type of result possible? Well, five things came to mind:

- Done is better than perfect
- Redirecting after accepting mistakes
- Focus
- Fun
- Growth mindset

DONE IS BETTER THAN PERFECT

Psychologists Thomas Curran and Andrew Hill studied more than 40,0000 people from 1989 to 2016 and found that perfectionism has increased by 33% since 1989. We seem to be internalizing a myth that life should be perfect when, in fact, that is an impossible outcome.

The research shows those who become preoccupied with perfection set themselves up against challenges.

The key to moving ahead is to follow through, and our associates performed exceptionally well during this crisis.

Redirecting after accepting mistakes
So, you made a mistake, now what?

- Recognize that sinking feeling
- Assess: what happened and why
- Make it right
- Adjust the system or process
- Be kind to yourself.

"If you don't make mistakes, you're not working on hard enough problems. And that's a big mistake."

~ F. Wikzek

Curiosity is the art of questioning everything without judgment or assumptions. With this approach comes continuous improvement and learning. As I look at our associates, they have a mindset of constant improvement. They participate in an ecosystem that encourages life-long learning, sharing, and best practices.

FOCUS
The human brain is programmed to narrow its concentration in the face of a threat. We are designed for self-protection.

The trap is that your field of vision becomes restricted. Leaders need to intentionally pull back, opening our mental aperture to take in the mid-ground and background.

As a veteran, it's what we call - situational awareness — taking a broader view of both challenges and opportunities.

During this crisis, we've provided our associates with clear communication on:

- What was
- What is
- And what will be

There was a past of relative stability and predictability. There now is disruption and uncertainty. There will be a different future state. As this future unfolds, our associates are preparing to be resilient. To be gritty. That's a competitive advantage.

FUN

According to a 2015 study, laughing makes us more open to new people and helps us build relationships. And real estate sales are a relationship business.

We booked a virtual comedy night in the quarantine and a virtual American Idol knock off event. Laughter can improve our health and make us better learners. And what's more: laughter is contagious.

GROWTH MINDSET

The truth is we all have our fixed-mindset triggers. When we face challenges, receive criticism, or compare ourselves with others, we can easily fall into insecurity and defensiveness, a response that inhibits growth.

To spend more time in a growth zone, our team and associates have worked hard in small groups to identify the triggers that do not serve us. It's hard work, yet it pays off.

During the quarantine, our most effective associates during this crisis followed a pattern:

- They controlled the controllable
- They prepared, planned, and trained
- They had situational awareness
- They kept the human factor in mind
- They guarded their mind & heart

At the end of the day, they ensured their choices reflected their hopes and not their fears. You can do the same.

#WinTheDay

3 WAYS TO SURVIVE AND THRIVE

"We thrive not when we've done it all, but when we still have more to do."

~ Sarah Lewis

Have you ever wondered if our response to hardship and failure ultimately determines success in life?

How is that some people release their survival mentality and embrace the opportunity to use hardships to heal, grow, and help out while others do the opposite? In this article, I intend to deliver three ways to move from survival to thriving.

MODEL OTHERS

At its core, all businesses are just people carrying out an idea, solving a problem for a profit. It's never the other way around; for instance, there is no idea so big that it doesn't need people to make it succeed. Investors know this, hence the saying "Bet on the jockey, not the horse." A great jockey is a great role model.

The tale of two real estate agents... in one of our nearby communities, a real estate agent is suing the local municipality over the shelter in place restrictions. The mayor posted – naming the agent – that at this time, he is having to redirect his energy and resources to the lawsuit rather than be entirely devoted to the crisis. The community is "virtually running the agent out of town" while slamming him all over social media that he cares more about selling homes than the city.

I'm not judging here; as citizens, it is our right to use the legal system… it's not about right or wrong. Who knows, maybe the agent will win the battle, yet you and I know he has already lost the war. I would not model my business after this agent.

Contrast this to James Sharp, one of our JPAR top producers based in Plano, Texas. James and his team have adapted quickly to virtual showings, virtual listings and becoming resourceful in advising buyers and sellers on what they can do in this market like:

- Continue to work virtually on mortgage pre-approval
- Virtually consult with him and other professionals
- Continue to research and stay informed
- View listings online
- Giving back - serving the community where there is a need

A perfect model to thrive in today's market. What makes me proud of our JPAR associates is I could name 100 others – like James – that have emailed, texted, or shared via zoom how they are serving their communities at this time while still virtually serving the needs of existing clients.

CREATE HOPE

Those of you who know me personally know that one of my favorite quotes is:

"Once You Choose Hope, Anything Is Possible."

In his book "The Hope Quotient," Ray Johnston reveals a revolutionary new method for measuring and dramatically increasing your level of hope.

Hope is more than a feeling; it's the by-product of seven key factors. When these factors are present in your business, they cause hope to thrive.

Factor 1: Recharge Your Batteries.
Nobody does well running on empty.

Factor 2: Raise Your Expectations.
You don't get what you deserve; you get what you expect.

Factor 3: Refocus on the Future.
It's time to throw away your rearview mirror. No one goes forward well when they have an unhealthy obsession with looking back.

Factor 4: Play to Your Strengths.
Be yourself; everyone else is taken.

Factor 5: Refuse to Go It Alone.
Never underestimate the power of support. Even the Lone Ranger had Tonto.

Factor 6: Replace Burnout with Balance.
Burning the candle at both ends isn't as bright as you think.

Factor 7: Play Great Defense.
Avoid the five toxic hope killers that can threaten your future.

What are those 5 Hope Killers?

1. Bitterness and resentment
2. Worry and anxiety
3. An unhealthy obsession of looking back and comparing
4. Guilt
5. Past failures

What practical steps can you take to improve your defense?

1. Never make big decisions when you're down.
2. Respond to bad news in resourceful ways.
3. Shake it off and step up.

Johnston explains how building these seven factors of hope into your life will dramatically increase your hope level and free you, and fuel you to catch a fresh vision for your future. And when that happens, anything is possible.

Now fair warning if you go to buy the book, Johnston is a devout Christian. I believe in our constitution and the freedom of religion – it's one of many things that makes America great. Now I'd like to share I have friends and associates from every faith and of no faith. I respect their freedom, and they respect mine.

BUILD RESILIENCE

"More than education, more than experience, more than training, a person's level of resilience will determine who succeeds and who fails. That's true in the cancer ward, it's true in the Olympics, and it's true in the boardroom."

~ Diane Coutu

According to Coutu, resilient people possess three characteristics:
- A staunch acceptance of reality;
- A deep belief and associated values that life is meaningful;
- An uncanny ability to improvise.

She states, you can bounce back from hardship with just one or two of these qualities, but you will only be truly resilient with all three. These three characteristics hold true for resilient organizations as well.

Coutu says that resilience is a reflex, a way of facing and understanding the world that is deeply etched into a person's mind and soul.

Resilient people and companies face reality with staunchness, make meaning of hardship instead of crying out in despair, and improvise thin air solutions. Others do not. This is the nature of resilience!

There are more than three ways to survive and thrive, yet a good start is finding great role models, creating more hope, and building your resilience.

Let's get started today!
#WinTheDay

WHAT TO DO NEXT?

"Where the focus goes, the energy flows."

~ Tony Robins

Jack Canfield said it best: You only have control over three things in your life:

1. The thoughts you think,
2. The images you visualize, and
3. The actions you take.

How you use these three things determines everything you experience.

Decide what you want; create a compelling reason why you want it; find an accountability partner; stay committed vs. just interested; execute your plan with passion; remain flexible yet focused and finally celebrate the small wins along the way.

I'd leave you with the exercise, with this action plan for today:

Think about what the next five years, the next ten years look like for you. When you stand there and look back at today, who do YOU NEED TO BE to make that happen?

BE that person today!

#WinTheDay

WHAT WE CAN LEARN
FROM LOUIS PASTEUR

**Let me tell you the secret that has led me to my goal. My
strength lies solely in my tenacity.**

~ Louis Pasteur

Authors note: this was written some 12 months before the
COVID-19 challenge. It was timely then and timely now.

Friday night reading – you know I love breakthrough stories.

I knew Louis Pasteur was the father of microbiology and
known for his discoveries of the principles of vaccination,
pasteurization, and the causes and prevention of diseases. I
knew his findings have saved many lives. I didn't realize the
sacrifice, the danger, and the obstacles he had to overcome:

- To find the cure for rabies, he had to endure working with
  mad dogs and overcome extreme doubt about the first test
  injection;
- He was mocked and ridiculed for suggesting hand washing
  to prevent infection and the spread of disease. It took 19
  years before that practice was widely accepted;

- One of his colleagues died helping stop the spread of cholera in Egypt; he wrote, **"he died on the battlefield of science passing through this life with a higher thought to which he sacrificed all else."**

Most of us aren't solving such complex problems, yet similar obstacles impact whatever we are trying to accomplish.

What I learned from Louis is:
- Despite his doubts and fears, he continued to take action
- Despite the confusion, lack of clarity, he kept moving forward
- He stepped backed to gain perspective vs. becoming overwhelmed
- He became resourceful, seeking out the necessary help
- He distanced himself from any drama
- He stayed focused on his commitments despite his feelings
- He developed and refined a growth mindset

My biggest takeaway is:

Take consistent positive action forward despite your fears and doubts.

#WinTheDay

UNPRODUCTIVE BUSYNESS, BAD FOR YOU!

Unproductive busyness, bad for you and bad for your business.

Have you ever noticed the vacation syndrome? That is where you get more done in the two days before you go on a vacation that you accomplished in the last two weeks. Can you relate?

Parkinson's law:
Work increases to fill the time available.

Pareto (80/20):
Extra time fills with unimportant activities.

The solution?
Ask yourself – How would you get your work done tomorrow if:

• You only had 2 hours per day to complete it?
• You only had 2 hours per week to complete it?

Then, write down only 2 mission-critical items and test by asking:

- Would I be satisfied with my day if only that happened?
- What are the consequences if they don't?

Complete those tasks by 11 AM the next day.

Don't multitask.

#WinTheDay

THE PROBLEM WITH THE
TRADITIONAL TO-DO LIST

Outcomes matter.

The problem with the traditional to-do list is that it's about tasks and not about outcomes. An outcome could be something like:

"increase revenue by 25%" or "build a relationship with specific people."

There is no single task that will cause the outcome. There is arguably a set of functions that could build-up to it.

Concrete, measurable outcomes are better than vague ones, but some highly desirable outcomes can only be qualitatively stated (like relationships) and cannot be quantified (like the number of appointments).

So, for myself, I am working to get better at linking my daily tasks to the outcome via process goals. More importantly, I am also trying to nail down this art of defining the process that leads to the desired outcome.

For some of you, that might be 3 or more NEW appointments each week. So I'd rather see something like this:

Create 3 or more new appointments each week... then list the task, the process to support that outcome.

Creating 2 or more closings per month between now and the end of the year and then list the associated process will lead to appointments that will lead to signed agreements.

Deepen my relationship with 4 people... then list people and the process that will achieve that outcome

Make sense?

What are your key outcomes and associated processes for this week?

#WinTheWeek

WHAT WOULD HAPPEN: IF YOU NEVER TOLERATED INACTION?

You don't have to be great to start, but you have to start to be great.

~ Joe Sabah

This week I had the opportunity to speak with several real estate agents about their upcoming New Years' resolutions. Research has shown that about half of all adults make New Year's resolutions. However, fewer than 10% manage to keep them for more than a few months. Like me, does this statistic make you wonder why?

What's the solution?

CONSIDER THIS:
What would happen if, starting today, you never tolerated inaction in yourself? Think about that for a moment again; what would happen if, starting today, you never tolerated inaction in yourself?

From the book Atomic Habits, there is a common mistake that often happens to too many of us. The error has to do with the difference between **_being in motion and taking action_**. They sound similar, but they're not the same.

When you're in motion, you're planning and strategizing and learning. Those are all good things, but they **_don't produce a result_**. Action, on the other hand, is the type of behavior that will **_deliver an outcome._**

Here's a couple of practical examples:
- If I outline 20 ideas for articles I want to write, that's motion.
- If I write and publish an article, that's action.
- If I email 10 new leads for my business and start conversations with them, that's motion.
- When I set an appointment, that's action.
- If I search for a better diet plan and read a few books on the topic, that's motion.
- If I eat a healthy meal, that's action.

Sometimes motion is useful, yet it will never produce an outcome by itself. It doesn't matter how many times you talk to the personal trainer; that motion will never get you in shape. Only the action of working out will get the result you're looking to achieve.

If the motion doesn't lead to results, why do we do it?

Sometimes we do it because we need to plan or learn more. But more often than not, we do it _because motion allows us to feel like we're making progress_ without running the risk of failure. Most of us are experts at avoiding criticism. It doesn't feel right to fail or to be judged publicly, so we tend to avoid situations where that might happen. And that's the biggest reason why you slip into motion rather than taking action: ***you want to delay failure.***

It's easy to be in motion and convince yourself that you're still making progress. You think, *"I've got conversations going with four potential clients right now. This is good. We're moving in the right direction."* Motion makes you feel like you're getting things done. But really, you're just preparing to get something done. When preparation becomes a form of procrastination, you need to change something. You don't want to be planning merely. You want to be practicing.

SOME IDEAS TO GET OUT OF MOTION AND INTO ACTION:
1. **Work expands to the time you give it:** Set a specific time for each task.
2. **Set a schedule for your actions:** Basic time blocking.
3. **Pick a date to shift you from motion to action:** set hard deadlines.
4. **Switch your feelings:** "I don't feel like it" to "Let's get this done!"

For some goals, setting a daily or weekly schedule doesn't work as well. This is the case if you're doing something that is only going to happen once: studying for your broker exam or getting your GRI. These things require some planning upfront (motion). They also need plenty of action to complete them. For example, you could set a schedule each week to study. In a situation like this, research shows it's best to pick a date. Put something on the calendar – like the test date. Make it public. This is when X is happening. In other words, set a HARD DEADLINE.

Research shows that people who make a specific plan for when and where they will perform a new habit are more likely to follow through. Too many people try to change their habits without these necessary details figured out. We tell ourselves, "I'm going to eat healthier" or "I'm going to write more," but we never say when and where these habits will happen. We leave it up to chance and hope that we will "just remember to do it" or feel motivated at the right time.

Hope is not a strategy!

An implementation intention sweeps away foggy notions like "I want to work out more" or "I want to be more productive" or "I should vote" and transforms them into a concrete plan of action.

Many people think they lack motivation when what they lack is clarity.

A straightforward way to apply this strategy to your habits is to fill out this sentence:

I will [BEHAVIOR] at [TIME] in [LOCATION]

- I will follow up with 4 leads a day for 30 minutes at 9 a.m. in my office.
- I will complete part 1 of my project, investing twenty minutes at 10 a.m. in my office.
- I will exercise for one hour at 5 p.m. at my gym.
- I will make my wife a cup of tea at 7 a.m. each morning in the kitchen.

Give your habits time and space. The goal is to make the time and location so apparent that, with enough repetition, you get an urge to do the right thing at the right time, even if you can't say why.

To put it: planning out when and where you will perform a specific behavior turns your environment into a trigger for action. The time and place trigger your behavior, not your level of motivation.

Motivation is short-lived and doesn't lead to consistent action. If you want to achieve your goals, you need a plan for exactly *when* and *how* you're going to execute them regardless of how you feel.

There are some lessons that only failure can teach. Failure is not the problem… inaction is… procrastination is.

Let's commit this week to move from motion to action.

#WinTheDay

KNOWLEDGE MINUS
ACTION = NOTHING

God provides the wind, but man must raise the sails.

~ St. Augustine

K minus A equals 0
K plus A equals W

K = knowledge
A = Action
W = Winning

I've coached a few folks that told me, "I want to produce more… my desire is to be more consistent." Some have been saying this for way too long. Why… fear.

Fear keeps our behavior inconsistent with our goals.

Those of you that know me know I'm a life-long learner. Although I agree with life-long learning, I agree much more with a life-long application – taking action – on what we're learning.

At The End Of The Day, The Winners Are The Doers.

Figure out where you want to go, start with the end in mind, and work your way backward to the moment at hand.

For example, what would happen if, for every 12 people you know, you set a system to touch them 33 times throughout the year? Could that "system" create 1 new transaction for every 12 people in your database?

What would happen if you added 1 new contact to your CRM everyday… and that contact was then touched 8 times in the first 8 weeks of meeting them and then 33 times during the next year? What would happen?

Here's the best of the blog series, the highest engaged post about taking action:

Number 1:
5 Lessons From The Death Crawl Scene In "Facing the Giants."

Too often, our perception, surroundings, and beliefs get in the way of victory and success. Or, another way, the meaning we assign to things becomes the lens through which we see the world.

Number 2:
What Would Happen If You Never Tolerated Inaction In Yourself?

There is a common mistake that often happens to too many of us. The error has to do with the difference between being in motion and taking action. They sound similar, but they're not the same.

Number 3:
Tired Of Not Getting What You Want?

Ever wonder why so many of us have to hit rock bottom before we find a breakthrough?

Number 4:
If Information Was Enough…

If information was enough, we would all be top performers in our profession, exercise every day, eat more vegetables, be within the government height and weight standard, and have a ton of money saved for the future.

Number 5:
3 Steps to Mastery

Who doesn't want to be a better agent, better team leader, a better entrepreneur? If there is one concept that can lead to more powerful performance with immediate impact… this is it: "It's difficult to control our thoughts and feelings, yet we have total control of our actions."

In summary, information overload creates a lull in productive activity, so let's look at three simple, fuss-free steps to get you the results you need:

Step 1: Move beyond the learning phase. While knowledge is a powerful thing, don't make the mistake of thinking your good intentions count. It's time to stop procrastinating and trust the tools you have to start taking positive steps.

Permit yourself to execute on the things you know now... nothing good happens when you wait.

👣 **Step 2:** Skip out on perfection. Perfection is a stall tactic. Typically, nothing big and drastic needs to happen in your routine. Small changes are what count.

Just take action, now!

👣 **Step 3**: Execute an action plan. Knowledge is only power when combined with action.

What actions can I take?

Here's one approach to consider:

Daily
- 5 or more check-in calls that create 1 or more appointments
- 3 or more personal notes
- 1 addition to your database with an "8 touch campaign" over the next 8 weeks

Weekly
- Grab a beverage of choice with a top client or prospect that creates 1 or more new appointments
- Host at least 1 business to business networking session
- Complete 7 pop-bys that create 1 or more new appointments
- At least one video about local events or local market conditions

Monthly
- Start of the month and mid-month send a report of value to your database – with video content that creates appointments

- Targeted FB or Google ads that create appointments
- Strategic text messages to an opt-in database that create appointments

Knowledge plus action is power.

Figure out where you what to go, start with the end in mind, and work your way backward to the moment at hand.

#WinTheDay #GSD

PERSISTENCE – ALL THE REWARD IS IN THE FOLLOW UP!

"Do not fear failure but rather fear not trying."

~ Roy T. Bennett

These statistics will shock and surprise you. So, get ready. We recently did a blind study on incoming leads.

85% of the new leads received a follow-up, 15% got crickets.

So, what is the psychology of the 15% of sales professionals that never follow up on a new lead? Even more shocking is we found that of the 85% that did make the initial follow up, only 25% made a second attempt! And of that 25%, only 12% made a third attempt. So what's going on here?

It's the voice inside your head. It's a growth vs. fixed mindset.
- 2% of sales are made on the first contact
- 5% of sales are made on the third contact
- 10% of sales are made on the fourth contact
- 80% of sales are made on the fifth to twelfth contact

Persistence is the key to your success. In a study specifically related to real estate sales, sales professionals that made three attempts vs. those that made five or more attempts had more than a $100K difference in annual income.

Today we are bombarded with information. We are in information overwhelm. But that does not mean someone doesn't want to buy, sell or invest. It might be, like me, right now, it isn't a high priority.

Staying connected is the key. Using content from tools like Keeping Current Matters can help, yet so can a simple check-in call, text, or video chat.

It's you vs. your baby, and nothing is in your way except for your growth vs. fixed mindset.

#WinTheDay

REDESIGNING YOUR COMFORT ZONE

A criminal was caught in the act, arrested, and sent to the king for his punishment. The king told him he had a choice of two punishments. One, he could be hung by a rope. Or two take what's behind the big, dark, scary, mysterious door.

The criminal quickly decided on the rope. As the noose was being slipped on him, he turned to the king and asked: "By the way, out of curiosity, what's behind that door?"

The king laughed and said: "You know, it's funny, I offer everyone the same choice, and nearly everyone picks the rope."

"So," said the criminal, "Tell me. What's behind the door? I mean, I won't tell anyone," he said, pointing to the noose around his neck.

The king paused then answered: **"Freedom**, but it seems most people are so afraid of the unknown that they immediately take the rope."

Is fear getting in your way?

Is fear keeping you inside your comfort zone?

Does this self-talk track sound familiar?
- What if I fail?
- What if it does not work?

What is possible with a new self-talk track?

- What if it DOES work?
- What's the worst thing that can happen?
- What steps can I take?

You see, nothing BIG happens when you wait. Nothing BIG happens when you stay inside your comfort zone.

Are you too comfortable being comfortable?

Is it time to re-design your comfort zone?

You can never become an expert in working for sale by owners; you'll never get better at capturing expired listings, on-line leads, geography farming, or open houses by staying comfortable. To become an expert in these things, you must get comfortable being uncomfortable.

Eight steps to consider in getting more comfortable being uncomfortable:

1. Take nothing for granted.
2. Switch up your routine.
3. Move toward your fears.
4. Give up control.
5. Try something new until you feel comfortable.
6. Ask the questions that other people won't ask.
7. Start conversations with strangers, with more people.
8. Agree to something you wouldn't normally consider.

Fear is a natural and essential part of growth. Every time we consciously choose to step outside of our comfort zone, the next uncomfortable thing becomes a little bit easier.

What will you choose today, the uneasiness of uncomfortableness, or the comfort of the status quo?

#WinTheDay

THE RECIPE.
INGREDIENTS FOR YOUR
REAL ESTATE PRACTICE

Warning this is a long one, full of nuggets. It may take a few passes to pick up the points that apply to you and your current situation.

As we head into this Thanksgiving week, many of you have probably started putting together your shopping list to prepare your favorite family recipes. Perhaps some of you have even already fought the grocery store lines while others cross their fingers that the store will be open on Thanksgiving morning to get the last-minute missing ingredients.

While you balance the thoughts of the pending home invasion of long-lost relatives to your personal desires to increase your productivity from 0 to 20 after being inspired by Travis Robertson's motivational lessons.

Whether you're the one who has already fought the grocery store line and has their business plan in its final review, or you are secretly dreading putting pen to paper to write out next year's goal and all the while are hoping there is enough butter to make grandma's famous mashed potatoes, here is a "recipe" to win your new year.

Are you interested in GROWTH or COMMITTED to growth?

As you think about it, your favorite dishes more than likely aren't just thrown together but have been perfected over time. Everything is deliberate, from heating the oven to adding the extra teaspoon of ground pepper to the final cooling time. Your real estate practice is the same way.

What is your real estate business secret recipe? Perhaps you don't have one or are just looking to perfect your own. Unlike grandma, I'm here to share my *"secret,"* but not so secret recipe for success.

Before you even begin to cook, you will need to pull the recipe out, read it over a time or two, and prepare a plan of action. What ingredients do you need to shop for, when will you start the oven to ensure the food is prepared and ready in time for Aunt Mildred to show up fashionably 30 minutes late.

 Step 1: Mindset And Time Management

"What Would Happen When You Shift Your Focus?"
Stephen Covey wrote a great book about how to put first things first. My biggest learning was *"understanding that increasing my personal productivity is a process, not a destination."* Where are you spending the majority of your time? Are you spinning your wheels doing a not urgent and not important task because it's easier or maybe you just don't have to face a dreaded phone call that is urgent but unfortunately bearing bad news? What adjustments need to be made? Take a step back today and look at what activities are capturing your attention and what you

have pushed aside. Perhaps you need to reorient yourself and focus on that task or even hire someone to do it that you can manage. Or else you need to eliminate the fluff that has had your undivided attention.

The next step in the preparation is looking at your mindset. "Do You Have A Fixed Or A Growth Mindset?"

As nouns, the difference between mindset and attitude are clear: mindset is a way of thinking, while attitude is how that mindset shows up in your approach, language, the position of the body, or way of carrying yourself.

To illustrate, remember the story of the tortoise and the hare? The hare was so certain that he would win that he sat down and went to sleep during the race. The tortoise just plodded on and kept going, always thinking that he had a chance of winning. When the hare woke, he started running as fast as he could, but he was just too late: the tortoise had won.

The hare had a fixed mindset. He believed that his innate ability would always mean that he would win whatever he did.

The tortoise had a growth mindset. He believed that he needed to work hard and keep going if he was to win. He was also not afraid of failure or he would never have agreed to race the hare.

Develop that growth mindset to get on the winning track. Now that you have developed your mindset, you can start heating up. Do this by warming the oven, or in real estate terms, develop yourself before you even begin to combine the ingredients or in this case, work with clients.

Step 2: Preheat The "Oven" With Product Knowledge

Product Knowledge

A common trait among all top producers, they know the market. Success leaves clues, you need to know as much about your product as possible. Know the current inventory of properties offered for sale or lease. Spend time learning the different aspects of the neighborhoods and surroundings in the areas in which you have the most business. Be confident in your knowledge of the product. Know more about it than any of your competition and it becomes a differentiator. Constant challenge agents and brokers have is being different, as Seth Godin says, *"Be different, or charge less."*

While the oven is preheating and you're filling your head with market knowledge, you need to look over your entire recipe and lay out all your ingredients. Perhaps there are steps that overlap, but you want to make sure you're ready to execute multiple steps at the right time. You need to have a mindset when you go into the next step.

 Step 3: Combine Your Winning Ingredients

- 1 cup of Passion & Strategy
- 2 Tbsp Selling Skills
- 3 tsp Marketing Skills
- 4 cups Sweat & Financial Equity
- 1 cup Passion & Strategy

All the product knowledge in the word won't serve you or your clients if you lack passion. 'Passion' is a word so excessively used and almost always blindingly paired with work, that if you actually ask around you may find that not everyone really gets what passion is. At the root of it all, it points to that strong emotion you have inside of you, for someone, or something. And anyone who has ever succeeded in making a name for themselves would probably state their passion as a reason for their success, but do you know yours?

When it comes to passion – a strong emotion of desire – there is a need to be brave enough to both acknowledge and embrace it. Some let their passion take over the wheel and do things that challenge the status quo, push boundaries, wreck tradition and ultimately reshape the world as we knew it. To strive for your passion is to be different from the rest.

Yet we know _passion is NOT a strategy_. We can name political battles, wars and other activities where both sides were passionate about their cause yet LOST. Consider implementing these strategies in your business so that you can see massive growth and maximum success this year.

- The Planning Strategy: Create a business plan — and actually work it.
- The Reconnection Strategy: Reconnect with your sphere of influence and stay connected.
- The Social Strategy: Tighten up your social media.

2 Tbsp Selling skills… knowing what and how you say it matters
There is a subtle art to influence and persuasion, especially in the emotionally charged residential real estate sales world. It is essential to be looking for the lessons in your exchanges with others. Become a "student of engagement." Our unique B.A.N.K. code training helps you master engagement.

Developing trusting relationships requires continuing engagement, which helps build human trust and confidence, so essential to real estate transactions. Not all of your database needs to hear from you every day, but contacts do need to hear from you based upon the depth of your relationship and their need for your services. And don't forget the friends of your contacts, referrals have always and continue to be one of the strongest ways to earn new business.

3 tsp Marketing Skills

I've seen so many struggling teams and solo agents trying to "brand themselves" into the business using passive and influence strategies. It simply won't work. Marketing a physical product is much different than marketing a professional service.

Professional services respond to direct response marketing, like "Curious About The NEW value of your home? Find out by..." With a clear and concise "call to action" CTA you will gain your fair share of appointments and sales.

4 cups Sweat & Financial Equity

I don't know your current financial situation, yet I know if you have read this far, you desire to grow your business. And whether you have no money or lots of money it doesn't matter.

What matters is your RESOURCEFULNESS and your commitment. We just released to our JPAR family, a video training on 6 lead generation strategies you can execute today with ZERO dollars. Resourceful people are imaginative, proactive, open-minded and persistent.

I knew an agent once that was dead broke, she printed a bunch of Zillow Zestimates by addresses in her area, walked around and handed them out with a handwritten note that said "I wonder if this is accurate? Let's talk to find out." That's creative, resourceful and cost her only her time and a few low-cost materials. And yes, it created a business.

At the same time, dumping money into any new shiny marketing opportunity or lead source is worth nothing if you don't act upon it. You could have all the financial equity in the world, but if you don't put the sweat in the investment was a poor one.

Now you have mixed all the ingredients and are ready to pour it in the pan. A bowl of batter is just that before it's poured into a pan to be molded into a cake. It bakes because of the adversity it faces in the heat of things. In real estate, you will grow by jumping into the heat and working with your clients. But just as any good chef that knows the heat of the oven before they put their dish (or any wannabe that just doesn't want to burn dinner) you need to know your clients.

Step 4: Prep The Pan And Know Your Client's And Your Personality

Understanding your B.A.N.K. code and how to use it
Would you feel more comfortable going in for a listing presentation if you knew the homeowner highly valued numbers and formulas or if they prefer not to talk about how the sausage is made but rather how much of an emotional connection they have to their home and how they want to pass it on to the next "first time homeowner?"

87% of real estate sales professionals don't feel adequately prepared for sales calls and 66% of customers are turned off by most buyer and listing presentations—all because many of us struggle to effectively communicate the value of our offer, your promise. B.A.N.K.'s personality sales method helps you beat the odds and master the science of communication, negotiation, and closing more sales for increased revenue that will transform your life.

Your EQ is higher than your IQ

In his 1996 book Emotional Intelligence, author and psychologist Daniel Goleman suggested that EQ (or emotional intelligence quotient) might actually be more important than IQ. Why? Some psychologists believe that intelligence standards are too narrow and do not encompass the full range of human intelligence.

We all understand the IQ test… yet EQ, on the other hand, is a measure of a person's level of emotional intelligence. This refers to a person's ability to perceive, control, evaluate, and express emotions. Researchers have helped shine a light on emotional intelligence, making it a hot topic in areas ranging from business management to education. EQ is centered on abilities such as:

- Identifying emotions
- Evaluating how others feel
- Controlling one's own emotions
- Perceiving how others feel
- Using emotions to facilitate social communication
- Relating to others

If you knew how to communicate with your sellers effectively and how to interact with them on an emotional level, how much further along would you be than the next agent

The time has come to put your dish in the oven, it's time to execute!

 Step 5: Execution

Execution

A business leader's job is to move forward and improve business performance successfully. This requires a continuous process of reflection, analysis, planning, and execution. There is no better way to learn/practice these skills than "by doing". It doesn't matter how good your strategies and tactics are if you don't execute them well it won't really matter. Much has been written about execution, and many tools and frameworks exist. One of our favorites is Franklin Covey's 4 Disciplines of Execution (4DX).

- Focus on the wildly important goal – WIG
- Act on the lead measures (levers you can influence)
- Keep a compelling/fun scoreboard (of lag & lead measures)
- Hold each other accountable (weekly reviews/commitments

If you have gotten to this point in our "recipe," your one step closer to meeting your goal. Now you have to commit to it. You have to commit to putting everything you have read above into action.

Commitment

Commitment requires being all in. If you are committed to your dreams and ambition, you prioritize and allocate time for action.

Commitment requires you to do whatever it takes whereas "interest" means you'll do just enough but not more. Entrepreneurs like you, are committed to the following traits:

1. Commit to being "all in" even if they don't know how to achieve the goal.

2. They take action with deep resourcefulness, trusting that they get outside of the box to find answers and resources.

3. Have beliefs, thoughts, and ideas that are congruent with the success of the goal.

4. Let go of needing approval and validation from others.

5. Invest fully in achieving the goal (like hiring a coach, expert and other support personnel.)

6. Address bottlenecks and roadblocks quickly. If there is a situation in the way that is stealing time or energy, committed goal-seekers will resolve the issues so they can get back to business.

7. Focus on the positive outcomes of achieving the goal instead of lamenting the cost of pursuing their dream.

8. Align goals to their values and priorities which creates limitless energy and inspiration during the pursuit.

9. Willing to get uncomfortable and take action (even though it might be scary) to achieve the goal.

10. Refuse to let any excuses be bigger than your commitment.

When you are committed, you will be relentless in your pursuit of the goal. Obstacles don't take you out of the game. They simply become a learning opportunity so that you get better at your game.

Conclusion

Some of you, if you have come this far – experienced, new and mid-career – are in survival mode at this very moment. It's hard to talk about your "why" or "passion" or the "recipe" of success when you are making rash decisions just pay the bills. In fact, for some of you it's hard to even think about planning for next week much less next year.

One solution to consider… find your sous chef or perhaps your Gordon Ramsay to motivate you in your kitchen. Perhaps there is a group of you in your first cooking class together or you're in advance pastry class, this is your tribe. They are the people who know you, who are rooting for you and are there to listen.

This can be a lonely business and having a community or a class of chefs behind you is how we were designed live and to thrive.

#WinTheDay

EXECUTION IS A NOUN!

Here is what I know, no book, no certification, no training course, no coaching program, or pill will EVER help you succeed as much as:

- The vision you see.
- The decisions you make.
- The beliefs you have.
- The peers you keep.
- The priorities you choose.

I'm often asked what the secret to the success of our top 1%:

EXECUTION
You see I know – and my team, knows – ideas are plentiful yet ACTION is the formula to make ideas successful.

So, my question today is, what's holding you back?

Nothing is particularly hard when it is broken down into smaller parts.

Are you ready to stop talking, thinking, stalling or getting ready to get to get ready?

Execution is a NOUN.

Once you know WHAT you want so many ask HOW? Yet before asking how ask yourself:

WHO DO I NEED TO BE?
Be that person now and the how will fall into place.
Let's GO!

#WinTheDay

ORGANIZATIONAL HABITS TO MAXIMIZE PRODUCTIVITY

What could you do with 11 more hours a week? A recent study by Unit4 indicated many of us loose up to 25% of our productivity each week due to a lack of streamlining our workflow or effectively using SMART phone applications.

Luckily for you and me, organization isn't an attribute you're born with, but a skill we can learn. And many of us can learn more! Proof? A poll by Office Depot found that 82% of people felt the more organized they were, the better they performed.

Here are five techniques to maximize your productivity, which one will you add to your portfolio this week?

Goals Up & Visual
Since you have invested time knowing and documenting what you want to achieve this year in your business and your personal life, why leave it hidden in a drawer or a closed book?

Out of sight quickly becomes out of mind. Up and visual is a proven technique to drive goal attainment.

Tip: Keep important information up and visible

18

There's An APP for that

While there is an APP for just about anything, many of us can benefit simply by using the basic functions of your SMART phone – Calendar, Notes, Reminders, and Voice Memo.

For example, setting reminders in your calendar for project deadlines. You can start with the deadline when the project must be completed and submitted, then work backward from there to set alerts for project components all along the way. You can even set additional notices to remind you to check on the progress, particularly if you are awaiting input from other people or teams. You'll never be caught off-guard by a huge project again.

Tip: Leverage your SMART phone Calendar; Notes; Reminders and Voice Memo.

Use the 80/20 Rule

When creating time blocks, use the 80/20 Rule to organize your schedule. The 80/20 rule is based around the idea that 20% of your work tends to produce 80% of your results. Productive workers identify their most important 20% tasks and organize their workday around getting them done first and foremost. The rest can be handled later or delegated, automated or eliminated.

Each time block contains a single task and an allotted amount of time for completing it. As we know, work EXPANDS to the time allotted! Scheduling your most essential tasks for the morning (or at those times when you're the most productive) is one habit the most productive have mastered.

For most of us reading this, your most productive time block is described with this acrostic: P.L.A.N. Prospecting,

Lead generation, Appointments (setting and going on), and Negotiations.

Creating new appointments is your MONEYBALL. Knowing the number of appointments needed to drive your goal and working backward is a high value 80/20 rule activity.

Tip: Time block your high leverage activities. Stay out of the whirlwind.

Adopt a System for Follow Up

In business, following up with leads and clients is crucial to success. All the money is in follow up. Lack of organized communication costs more than you think. A recent study showed that 2,000 real estate agents lost 55% of past clients' new business due to lack of follow up. Many real estate professionals have utilized customer relationship management systems (CRMs) that are used to follow up and keep leads, past clients, and other tasks focused and organized.

Tip: A strong focus on executing systems that make follow up a no brainer.

Multitasking is a big lie.

Contrary to popular belief, study after study shows that multitasking slows down a person's productivity rather than speeds it up. It can also lead to all-around subpar results.

Why?

When we multitask, our brains can't think in an organized way. We end up expending a lot of energy by switching our focus back and forth. Those that are highly productive recognize this and make it a habit to do one thing at a time. Even though their phone, for example, might be a vital part of your business, when something needs to get done, put all your focus – for a 45-minute time block - on the task at hand and put your device to the side in airplane mode. The same goes for all other distractors.

Tip: Singularity of focus for 45-minute time blocks
Peter Drucker said it best, "Nothing is less productive than to make more efficient what should not be done at all. Until we can manage our time, we can manage nothing else."

#WinTheDay

SMALL SHIFTS MAGNIFY OUTCOMES

I was recently reflecting on some coaching conversations and thinking about vectors. Let me explain:

In math and physics, a vector is a quantity having direction as well as magnitude, especially as determining the position of one point in space relative to another.

If a pilot makes the slightest one-degree error in the aircraft's flight path, after traveling one mile the plane will be off the course by 92 feet. And after going 60 miles, that error adds up to being a mile off the path.

A minor off course adjustment over time and distance magnifies the error. If a pilot were flying from New York to L.A. a one-degree shift in the flight path over the entire course would put the plane 40 miles to the South in Orange County at SNA not Los Angeles at LAX.

"The secret of your success is found in your daily routine. You alone are responsible for what you do, don't do, or how you respond to what's done to you." Darren Hardy, The Compound Effect

I work with a lot of entrepreneurs, and many times they call with a complete overall idea – overwhelmed and burned out – yet many times it's just the 1-degree change that compounds over time. Yes? Who can relate?

The compound effect, it works both ways.

What small course correction can you make this week?

#WinTheDay

WHAT IF TODAY WAS YOUR LAST?

Recently I read Steve Jobs commencement speech at Stanford in 2005. As you know, Steve was an American entrepreneur and business magnate. He was the Chairman, Chief Executive Officer (CEO), and a co-founder of Apple Inc., Chairman and majority shareholder of Pixar, a member of The Walt Disney Company's board of directors following its acquisition of Pixar, and the Founder, Chairman, and CEO of NeXT. Jobs is widely recognized as a pioneer of the microcomputer revolution.

What can we learn from Steve that applies to being the CEO of your real estate practice? Plenty. Read on:

When Steve was 17, he read a quote that went something like,

> **"If you live each day as if it was your last, someday you'll most certainly be right."**

It made an impression on him, and since then, for the past 33 years of his life, he looked in the mirror every morning and asked himself,

> **"If today were the last day of my life, would I want to do what I am about to do today?"**

And whenever the answer has been "No" for too many days in a row, he knows he needs to change something. A pattern interrupt.

Remembering that you'll be dead soon is the most crucial tool Steve Jobs ever encountered to help him make important life choices. Because almost everything — all external expectations, all pride, all fear of embarrassment or failure — these things just fall away in the face of death, leaving only what is truly important.

Remembering that you will die is the best way I know to avoid the trap of thinking you have something to lose. You are already naked. There is no reason not to follow your heart.

No one wants to die. Even people who – like me – want to go to heaven don't want to die to get there. And yet, death is the destination we all share. Our time, your time is limited, so don't waste it living someone else's life. Don't be trapped by dogma — which is living with the results of other people's thinking. Don't let the noise of others' opinions drown out your inner voice. And most important, dare to follow your heart and intuition. Somehow you already know what you truly want to become. Everything else is secondary.

So What's Holding You Back?

- What Action Have You Been Putting Off?
- What's The One Thing You Know, If You Took Action Today Would Make A Positive Impact On Your Business Or Your Personal Life?

Do that today, do it NOW as if today was your last.

#WinTheDay

BONUS SECTION

CALCULATING THE VALUE OF YOUR TIME WORKSHEET

"KNOW YOUR WORTH. NEVER SETTLE FOR LESS THAN YOU DESERVE."

IT'S TRUE, TIME IS MONEY!

In the real estate industry, knowing the worth of your time may not sound like an easy calculation. After all, agents all over the world focus their efforts on all sorts of things. Not too mention, REALTORS® have various business plans, models, and systems to identify and accomplish their goals within their set deadlines and hours of operation. However, many agents do not realize the importance of being able to analyze their time effectively to scale and drive productivity. Make no mistake, you're a business owner! Wouldn't it be nice to identify your worth down to the hour and minute? What if you could maximize the worth of your time by identifying and leveraging those tasks and functions that increase sales? Well, we've got good news!

The following exercise will help you identify your worth. Not only that, but you will be able to visually pinpoint the tasks and functions of your career that you should focus on, delegate, automate, or eliminate. Best of all, this is a simple exercise! No complex calculations or formulas are needed.

Let's get started!

MY HOURLY RATE

GCI (Gross Commissions Income) **Goal for the Year**

÷ **Number of Working Hours for the Year**

= $ _____ **My Hourly Rate**

Side note: There are 2080 hours in a 52 workweek business year (standard 40 hour work week, M-F). Your hourly rate will vary on your total hours for the year.

MY MINUTE RATE

$ _____ **My Hourly Rate**

÷ **60 Minutes**

= $ _____ **Per Minute**

X 10 $ _____ **Per 10 Minute**

X 15 $ _____ **Per 15 Minute**

X 30 $ _____ **Per 30 Minute**

X 45 $ _____ **Per 45 Minute**

THE TASKS & FUNCTIONS THAT EARN MORE THAN MY HOURLY RATE:

1. _____
2. _____
3. _____
4. _____
5. _____

These are the tasks & functions that contribute the most to closing more deals. Let's DOUBLE DOWN on these needle pushers!

THE TASKS & FUNCTIONS THAT EARN LESS THAN MY HOURLY RATE:

1. _____
2. _____
3. _____
4. _____
5. _____

These are the tasks & functions that do not substantially increase revenue & GCI. Let's DELEGATE, AUTOMATE, OR ELIMINATE these to maximize efficiency!

KNOW YOUR P.L.A.N.

When you know your **P.L.A.N.** everything else becomes clear! As the CEO of your real estate practice, your highest and best use is:

Planning - Do you have a business plan? What about systems and processes to stay on track? How are you keeping track of your progress and goals?

Lead Generation - What are you doing to produce a constant stream of leads? Where are your leads coming from (primary sources)? What is your conversion rate? CRM?

Appointment Creation - How many appointments must you set to meet your goals?

Negotiating - Are you negotiating with your buyers and sellers to close more deals? Do you need to brush up your negotiating skills? Have you acquired any certifications or designations to win the confidence of your clients and prospects?

THE ART & SCIENCE OF GOAL SETTING WORKSHEET

THE SCIENCE
OF SMART GOAL
SETTING

DON'T LET
EXCITEMENT
MORPH INTO
ANXIETY!

THE IMPORTANCE OF GOALS

Goals are like magnets that attract us to a higher ground and new horizons. They give our eyes a focus, our mind an aim, and our strength a purpose. Without their pull, we would remain forever stationary, incapable of moving forward.

A goal is a possibility that fulfills a dream.

You know the importance of setting goals... so why is it so hard to keep and reach them? We've all felt the excitement that comes with setting a new goal, but then, as time progresses, excitement can morph into anxiety. This is because we are facing the reality that we are so far from our goal and have no framework or strategy of how to get there.

So how do you overcome life's hurdles and personal mental roadblocks to reach your BIG goals?

The reality is that there's a SCIENCE to smart goal setting.

THREE TYPES
OF GOALS

👤👤👤 OUTCOME GOALS 1

An outcome goals is one that isn't really under your control. Instead, it's based on outside circumstances. For example, if your goal is to the #1 selling agent in your market, that's a goal that's not only based on your numbers, but also the numbers from other agents in your market too.

📈 PERFORMANCE GOALS 2

Performance goals are personal achievement goals. They are the building blocks that help you reach your outcome goal. A good performance goal example is to "beat my personal record of 21 homes sold in a year."

💭 PROCESS GOALS 3

Process goals are completely under your control and are composed of the things you do on a daily basis like habits and routines. Think of these as the small steps you take to get to your performance and outcome goals every single day. An example of a process goal would be to "spend 90 minutes prospecting daily" or "call 30 FSBOs every Monday."

THE SCIENTIFIC PROOF

In over 650 studies completed with over 50,000 participants, scientists analyzed what worked best when goal setting. Overall, individuals who focused on Process Goals had more success in reaching their goals than those who simply set Performance or Outcome Goals.

In addition, it was observed that specific and challenging goals are far more effective than vague goals of "trying to do your best." This is where SMART Goal Setting comes into play.

THREE TYPES
OF GOALS

👥 OUTCOME GOALS 1

An outcome goals is one that isn't really under your control. Instead, it's based on outside circumstances. For example, if your goal is to the #1 selling agent in your market, that's a goal that's not only based on your numbers, but also the numbers from other agents in your market too.

📈 PERFORMANCE GOALS 2

Performance goals are personal achievement goals. They are the building blocks that help you reach your outcome goal. A good performance goal example is to "beat my personal record of 21 homes sold in a year."

🧠 PROCESS GOALS 3

Process goals are completely under your control and are composed of the things you do on a daily basis like habits and routines. Think of these as the small steps you take to get to your performance and outcome goals every single day. An example of a process goal would be to "spend 90 minutes prospecting daily" or "call30 FSBOs every Monday."

THE SCIENTIFIC PROOF

In over 650 studies completed with over 50,000 participants, scientists analyzed what worked best when goal setting. Overall, individuals who focused on Process Goals had more success in reaching their goals than those who simply set Performance or Outcome Goals.

In addition, it was observed that specific and challenging goals are far more effective than vague goals of "trying to do your best." This is where SMART Goal Setting comes into play.

SMART
GOAL SETTING

SMART is an acronym that you can use to guide your goal setting. To make sure your goals are clear and reachable, each one should be:

Specific   SIMPLE | SENSIBLE | SIGNIFICANT

Measurable   MEANINGFUL | MOTIVATING

Achievable   AGREED | ATTAINABLE

Relevant   RELEVANT | REALISTIC & RESOURCED RESULTS BASED

Time Bound   TIME BOUND | TIME-LIMITED TIMELY | TIME-SENSITIVE

Here's a worksheet to use when setting your SMART Goals: (next page)

YOUR SMART GOALS WORKSHEET

NAME: _____

1. I want to achieve:

_____

2. My main MEASURE(S) for this achievement:
(E.G. what I will see, hear or feel when I have achieved the above)

_____

3. What I want to achieve stated as a SPECIFIC GOAL
(including my measures)

(Who) _____

(How) _____

(What) _____

(Where*) _____

(By When) _____

* It's not necessary to always state 'where'

4. To finish, run through the rest of the SMART Goal check list:
• Is what you want ATTAINABLE? Is it within your control to achieve it?
• Is it REALISTIC for you to achieve it?
• Is it TIMED?

You must answer 'YES' to all these questions. Change section 3 as necessary in order to do so.

SMART GOAL PLANNING

Now it's time to take action on your SMART goals. When planning your year, it's best to work from the outside in. Start by analyzing your big quarterly goals in all areas of your life, then moving closer and planning them out on a weekly and daily basis.

SMART GOALS
QUARTERLY PLANNER

NAME: _____

My Goals	Q1	Q2	Q3	Q4
Health & Fitness Goal				
Business Goals				
Relationship Goals				
Social Life Goals				
Personal Development Goals				
Financial Goals				
Quality of Life Goals				
Spiritual Goals				
Contribution Goals				

SMART GOALS
WEEKLY PLANNER

NAME: _____ WEEK/YEAR: _____

My Goals	My Action Steps This Week:	Success?	Learnings?
Health & Fitness Goal			
Business Goals			
Relationship Goals	Partner... Kids...		
Social Life Goals			
Personal Development Goals	Intellectual... Emotional...		
Financial Goals			
Quality of Life Goals			
Spiritual Goals			
Contribution Goals			

SMART GOALS
DAILY PLANNER

NAME: _____   TODAY'S DATE: _____

Goals to Work On	My Action Steps Today:	My Success	My Learnings
	7am		
	8am		
	9am		
	10am		
	11am		
	12pm		
	1pm		
	2pm		
	3pm		
	4pm		
	5pm		
	6pm		
	7pm		
	8pm		
	9pm		
	10pm		
	11pm		

HOW SMOOTH IS YOUR RIDE

HOW SMOOTH IS YOUR RIDE?

*It's NOT about being a perfect 10,
it's about creating a smoother ride!*

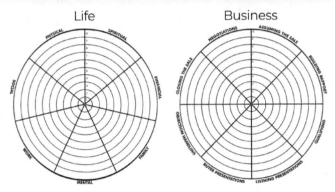

Life   Business

ABOUT THE AUTHOR

Mark is the host of "Success Superstars," a weekly show that highlights the blueprint of success, the co-founder of CoRecruit, and the Chief Executive Officer of JP & Associates REALTORS®, a rapidly growing full-service transaction-based real estate brokerage. He has invested nearly 25 years in understanding the inner workings of high performing real estate agents, teams, managers, and leaders in major markets across the world. Mark has served as a business coach in progressive leadership capacities for the 5th largest US-based real estate brokerage firm, in sales and customer marketing leadership capacities for a major consumer goods company, and served a stint in the US Army. He was later recalled to active duty during the desert storm campaign. Mark is a father of 3, a lifelong learner, Spartan, and adventure athlete. He earned his MBA from California State University and a Behavioral Change Certification from the National Association of Sports Medicine. Several years ago, he decided to make "One Helluva Move" and not play it safe, and since then, in his spare time, he has climbed the world' tallest free-standing mountain - Kilimanjaro; completed the Spartan trifecta, the LA Marathon, and the world-famous Iowa border to border RABGRAI ride among other crazy adventures.

Made in the USA
Middletown, DE
03 March 2021